ZEN POOL

AWAKEN THE MASTER WITHIN

MAX EBERLE

Copyright © 2007 by Max Eberle

ISBN 0-7414-4039-3

This Pool Player Logo is a TRADEMARK of Max Eberle and Max Eberle Products. All Rights Reserved.

Cover design by Max Eberle.

Published by:

INFI∞ITY
PUBLISHING.COM

1094 New DeHaven Street, Suite 100
West Conshohocken, PA 19428-2713
Info@buybooksontheweb.com
www.buybooksontheweb.com
Toll-free (877) BUY BOOK
Local Phone (610) 941-9999
Fax (610) 941-9959

Printed in the United States of America
Printed on Recycled Paper
Published August 2007

This Book is Dedicated to My Family, whose teaching, assistance, wisdom, love, and encouragement have greatly enriched my life and my journey on the path towards pool mastery.

ACKNOWLEDGMENTS

How does one say thank you when there are so many people to thank? If I forgot to thank you here please forgive me! Special thanks to my step-father, Tom Runge, who helped me edit this book and helped me in so many other ways while growing up. I give many thanks to those who have published my instructional articles and kept asking for more, which has in turn made this book possible. Thank you to JR Calvert and Sally Timko, my friends and the publishers of *Inside Pool* Magazine. They have a great magazine and are always out on the front lines of the pro pool scene helping to advance the sport. Thanks to my good friend Richard Schwary who has helped make Zen Pool possible.

Thanks to Carissa Biggs and Steve Lingelbach, my friends and publishers of *On the Wire* and the directors of the Pechauer Tour, keeping pool alive on the west coast. Thanks to my friends Lloyd Schonter and Terry Wachtell who got me to write my first columns for their monthly newsletter promoting the TAP Pool League which they founded. Thanks for the support and for inviting me to write a column in the first place.

Thank you to the pool masters in my life who have really taken an interest in sharing their knowledge with me. My grandfather Charles Eberle (1907-2002), my best friend and first and most influential teacher, what fun it was getting to know each other as he shared his depth of wisdom with me and believed in me all the way. Thank you to my father, Robert Eberle (1947-1989), for believing in me and telling me I can be anything I want. Thanks to my Uncle Dave Eberle for buying me pool books for my birthday and helping me to stop jumping up on my shots.

Thanks to Garten Bierbower of Ohio for showing me his amazing talent and vast knowledge of the game. I was blessed to play with and learn so much from one of the best pool players of all time. Thanks to Chan Whitt for teaching me what he knows even though I was a competitor of his late, great pool prodigy son Chan Whitt Jr... It was you who said "We want our opponents to be good; we don't want to go out and beat a bunch of slouches!" Chan Jr. was a true champion whose memory will live on forever. Thanks to my friend Nick Varner for being a great guy and for sharing his powerful mental outlook on competing. My gratitude to Jason Bowie for sharing his amazing sports and pool knowledge and for working with me to become a better athlete.

Thanks to Rich Lang, former owner of The Velvet Rail in Dover, OH, for giving me the keys to the pool hall so I could practice at all hours and to the current owner, my friend Steve Speer for always making me feel at home there. Thank you to my friends and fellow pros Charlie Williams, Danny Harriman, and Thorsten Hohmann. Thanks to Ralf Souquet, Oliver Ortmann, Thomas Engert, Steve Davis, and Efren Reyes. Thank you to Jeff Bey, owner of Hollywood Billiards and Tom Keller, a great photographer and one of the "nicest guys on the planet" who has done a lot of free and excellent work for me. Thank you to everyone who has ever helped or sponsored me on tour or in an event; Guy D'amecourt, Max Hoskins, Ralph Carlson, Scott Taylor, Chantal Burnison, Mohammed of Knight Shot in the UAE, Michael Winger Bearskin, Chris Corso, Paris Rain, Jim Burt, Robert Tobin, Garry Simmonds, Michael Gerard, Phil Muller, Dr. Paul Hyman, Chris and Shawn Carlson, Morgun Chang, Harrison Huff, Jesse Eaton, Andrew Park Custom Cues, Mike Howerton, Tim Hall, Ralph Rubin, Andy Scheinman, and Michelle Sass.

Thank you to Schaefer family: George, for setting up a European adventure, Mary Ann, Colby and John, one of my most inspirational friends. Thank you to Paul Kiel Smith and Jose Garriga Jr. Thanks to Bobby Higashi of Los Angeles for his friendship, support, and great conversations over lunch. Thanks Samm(antha) Diep and Chisolm Woodson, you rock!

Thanks to all of my family; my mother Estelle and father Rob, my second "mom" Loi Eberle, Bob Bissett, my brothers Stephen Eberle and Will Eberle, my beautiful little sisters Katie Runge and Emily Eberle, Ann Hardesty, Ed Hardesty, Matthew Hardesty, Alison Hardesty, Charles and Connie Eberle, Grandma Francis, and everyone who has ever helped me make it in life, there are so many more…you know who you are!

PREFACE

This book is a compilation of most of the instructional articles I have written for various pool and billiard publications over the last ten years. Most were written as an instructional staff member of *Inside Pool Magazine*, some for *On The Wire* (the West Coast Pool Newspaper), and the earliest ones for the TAP Pool League's monthly newsletter.

The title, Zen Pool, is at once a reflection of my approach to the game, a description of the nature and presentation of instruction contained in these pages, and a tribute to my mother Estelle. I remember one night as a teenager I was leaving the house to play a local 9-Ball tournament when my mom told me as I was heading out the door, "Zen Pool, Max, Zen Pool." Remembering these simple yet elegant words from my mother has often been helpful in reminding me to access a deeper part of myself while playing pool. Offering no explanation, she left it to me to interpret "Zen Pool" and extract value from the thought on my own.

The idea of Zen Pool describes my truest feelings about the game and gives a tangible thought available for positive use. If I am out of touch with my game, or if I want to improve upon a good playing session, the thought "Zen Pool" helps me get there.

The first article was written specifically for this book and is a deeper look into Zen and what Zen Pool means to me. The articles each have a singular main idea and each could be considered its own "Zen Meditation" for your pool game. However, they may also contain extra nuggets of helpful information. They are arranged randomly and not as a step-by-step program. There is information directed toward all levels of players, so you can search for answers based on the article title or just by reading the collection in any order you choose.

Since I have been a personal instructor for over fifteen years, many of the topics were inspired by common faults in play that I have consistently found in many of my students' games; faults that hinder better play for players everywhere. Many other topics were inspired not by faults in play but by a lack of information that, when learned, can greatly improve one's ability. The diagrams are my hand drawn artwork, as I have always enjoyed drawing pool diagrams, especially during classes at school.

Improving at pool consists both of an honest search for faults with a daily eagerness to work on correcting them, and the diligent gathering of new and useful knowledge. No matter how good you become, it is constructive to always consider yourself a student of the game.

I was in my early teens when my grandfather told me that there are many rungs on the ladder to improvement which get further apart and harder to reach the better you get. Dramatic improvement in the beginning seems easy and fast compared to the harder earned improvements as you reach the higher levels of play.

My intention with each article has been to provide a key rung on the ladder to improvement that a player can grab onto and pull himself up with to a higher level. Many of the ideas could also be considered foundational in that, once mastered, they open a whole new world of possibilities that would otherwise be unreachable.

Some of the articles may help just by reading and contemplating the ideas, while others present ideas or fundamentals that require many hours of focused and disciplined effort to integrate into your game. Pool, with all of its beauty and free rolling spheres, also has a precise geometrical nature that requires a high degree of technical body awareness and control. It can be amazing how fixing one detail in your fundamentals or implementing a new concept can improve your game.

While my own improvement is an ongoing process, I have applied the knowledge here to my own game with excellent results, including greater consistency and many match and tournament wins. My hope is that I have communicated clearly enough so that it helps you get what I believe you are looking for; real and lasting improvement…and more fun out of the game you love to play.

Here is my legendary pool champion Grandfather, Charles Eberle "Pop," when he was 92, and me when I was 27 in the year 2000. This was in the living room in the house that he built in Dover, Ohio. The pool table that got me hooked on the game was in the basement.

CONTENTS

INTRODUCTION

The desire to become a great pool player hit me at the age of twelve. This is when I really appreciated how well my grandfather played. I was amazed by his ability to control the cue ball and beat everyone in town. My father, uncle and cousins were good, too, and it was this environment that made my introduction to the game so enjoyable.

The result of the Dover, Ohio City Championships in the early eighties was my grandfather Charles Eberle–first place; my uncle Dave Eberle–runner-up; and my cousin Danny Eberle (Dave's son)–third place. I wanted a piece of the action, and I had people there who were willing to help.

I became a sponge of information and a machine in working on putting my new passion and knowledge into action. I *had* to master this game; there simply was no alternative that existed in my mind. This desire and obsession attracted me to some of the best teachers and players available who kindly showed me stuff which I was eager to learn.

The strong picture in my mind of what I wanted to accomplish also got me through the rough times, when my game seemed to stagnate, or go downhill, even when I was playing more than ever. These slumps would last a few days to a couple of weeks, and I could not stand to be playing so poorly after just having played so well. This would make me even more determined to succeed. It was during these slumps that I would always go back to the basics as I knew them, and search out better and cleaner ways of executing my shots and my form. I would always, without fail and much to my delight, come out of these slumps playing better than I ever had before. My confidence would soar and I would improve still more…and then another slump…and then more improvement. This process would keep repeating itself, and my game just kept better by leaps and bounds as time progressed.

In order to improve your game, all you must do is want it badly, believe it is possible, and go for it full tilt even when your results appear otherwise. You have got to be dedicated and willing to make changes that will help you in the long run.

As in any sport, developing and mastering your fundamentals is huge. Work on your fundamentals starts to become fun once you start to experience how much it really pays off.

In-depth knowledge is huge. Reading about the game and taking lessons is fun and worthwhile when you gain new insights that soon help you on the table. The process of improving itself becomes a joy as you start to really receive the benefits of your investigation and labor. When you achieve high levels of play and experience flashes of brilliance that turn the table into your playground and the cue ball into an extension of your mind, all of that hard work and perseverance somehow seems to be worth all the effort.

One who seeks enlightenment does not complain about the hardships entailed on the journey; rather, the difficulty becomes joy as he knows a prize worthy of achievement makes any trouble in attaining it miniscule by comparison.

Your author (shooting), maybe eight years old, playing in the basement in Dover, Ohio with older brother Stephen to the left. This pool table was our playground since we were little. We would chase each other around it, make a fort underneath it, and make up games rolling the balls around without using cues. Actually playing pool was a very adult thing to do on the table and watching our dad and grandfather play was always very serious. When I was twelve and my grandpa told me how to make a carom on the nine off of the 2 ball and it went in—I knew I had found my calling. My brother Stephen pursued music and became a great guitarist.

ZEN POOL

We all have a basic feeling for what Zen means. Zen is most often linked with the idea of meditation. With this in mind, bringing Zen into anything you do would be to add a deeper quality of meditative awareness into your activity.

The origin of Zen is Mahayana Buddhism, which is a major school of Buddhism which teaches compassion, universal salvation (everyone will become a Buddha), and enlightened wisdom. Zen is a branch of Mahayana Buddhism which strongly emphasizes the practice of moment-by-moment awareness and of 'seeing deeply into the nature of things' by direct experience. Zen thinking asserts that enlightenment can be attained through meditation, self contemplation, and intuition.

In this sense, playing pool is Zen in that it does require your present moment awareness, the enlightenment that comes from the accumulation of direct experience, and the contemplation of the many nuances which are inherent in your self and in the game.

According to the Hackers Dictionary of Computer Jargon at worldwideschool.org, Zen means: To figure out something by meditation or by a sudden flash of enlightenment. Originally applied to bugs, it occasionally applied to problems of life in general. "How'd you figure out the buffer allocation problem?" "Oh, I zenned it." In this sense you may discover a new shot or fix a problem in your game by "zenning it;" yet, for the most part, you will need to "Zen" every shot you face for a couple of reasons. One is that every shot is "something that needs to be figured out" (or at least worked out), and two because this will require at least some amount of concentration and awareness, no matter how easy or standard the shot appears. Having the attitude that every single shot you ever take is unique will help keep you to be present in what you are doing, a trait found in all great players.

Let us look into the direction of meditation, as Zen is directly related. Meditation usually refers to a state in which the body is consciously relaxed and the mind is allowed to become calm and focused. Often thought of as a form of alternative medicine, meditation brings about mental calmness and physical relaxation by suspending the stream of thoughts that normally occupy the mind.

Generally practiced by sitting quietly in a room with eyes closed for twenty or more minutes, it is used to reduce stress, alter hormone levels, and elevate one's mood. The idea is to pay attention to the inner silence instead of the outer or inner chaos. Ultimately, meditation brings you to a state of just "being" in the now and being receptive to what is available. This "being in the now" is the moment-by-moment awareness aspect of Zen and of playing Zen Pool. A mind cluttered with outer or inner chaos will find it difficult to direct the body into playing run out pool. However one will also need to use one's mind in playing pool, and this is the focus aspect that comes with meditation.

The dictionary defines meditate as: to plan or intend, or to think deeply (Webster's New World Dictionary, 2nd ed., Simon & Shuster, 1979, p. 299). If you are awake in "the now," you will have more mental energy available to plan what you intend to do on the table. Putting mental energy into planning will also help make useless thoughts disappear and bring you into the present moment.

Once you have made a plan and it is time to enact your shot-making process, you can use mental energy to help direct the physical process and allow your mind to be quieter in terms of thoughts and words—yet still be engaged with the eyes, body and the shot you face in creating the 'pre-meditated" outcome. This phase will be the playing out or expression of your plans. The better you are playing, the closer your results will be to your plans.

For a long time, I have called pool a form of meditation. To meditate requires no one but you. Playing pool also requires no one but you. If you are a person who does not like to play alone, I invite you to see the game differently and play alone for the benefits you will receive, and to find out just how challenging and fun the game is when you actually put effort into figuring it out. Similar to the benefits touted by meditation, I have often experienced a reduction of stress and an elevated mood after practice sessions and even tournament play.

One great thing about pool is that it requires a multi-dimensional awareness for your body, mind, and spirit. Knowing everything about pool will not help if you cannot control your body to make your plans happen. Knowing everything and being able to do it is also not enough if the motivation or "spirit" to do so is absent. There must be a certain amount of joy or desire in order to "Zen in" on playing the game. It is no accident that the greats of almost anything also happen to love doing it more than most people.

The physical aspect of playing pool is a dance that requires the coordination of your entire body. It is not only about hand-eye coordination; it is *hands*-eye coordination and even *body*-hands-eye coordination. This fact proves that pool is a sport along with the fact that it requires an accurate and sometimes powerful throwing motion. Not surprisingly, you will find that top pool players are gifted in other sports as well, and willing to train for countless hours, months, or years to perfect their technique.

Yet even if you are not a superstar athlete or do not intend on being a pro pool player, just the effort of attempting to improve your form will increase your own body awareness, help your game, and serve a yoga-like benefit to your life. The spirit you put into improving even a little bit could help your overall life spirit in accomplishing other things you wish to do in life. With a focused, calm, and awake mind, body and spirit, you will continually learn more and more and even develop your own understanding about what it means to play Zen Pool.

In describing Zen, I call it a meditative-like state in which one is at peace, balance and connection with one's self and one's surroundings. This place of calm makes the tools one possesses available in the moment. This place could often be considered quiet, yet it is possible to speak, make music or make noise from a Zen place or state of being. Zen is a place where you feel safe and can focus on something, whatever it is that interests you. Zen is where you can really look into something and find the beauty in the details.

Zen is a state of being where you can learn and master an art with the patience to get there in however long it takes, coupled with the keen interest to bring about a steady climb in one's knowledge and experience which usually leads to an increase in ability. So I call Zen a wakeful, mindful, present, peaceful state that one can be in during the midst of an activity or the learning about an activity or both.

To say peace is involved in Zen does not exclude the possibility for passion and intense focus in what one is doing. Focusing with passion on something we love to do is peaceful to our soul in the moment.

One of the purest forms of Zen I can think of in relation to pool is when I am totally aware and involved in what I am doing with my body and eyes and in the situation or shot that I am planning to make happen on the table. Whether planning my shot, setting up my stance, or delivering my stroke, I am all eyes, feel, and alertness to what is happening. I am in the moment, enjoying the process, working to succeed—yet not wondering about whether my desired result will happen. I keep in feel and in imagination the image of my shot while immersed in the process: aware, in control, and relaxed.

It is funny that when I am at my best and I miss the shot or miss position, I usually know what happened wrong just as the cue ball leaves the tip because my feel and awareness are so heightened that I knew exactly what went wrong in my shot process; what I did wrong or failed to do right. When I'm not at my top level and miss a shot, I may not be sure if the ball is going in or not and I may have to think or reflect a bit to figure out what the problem was. In the Zen state, you are on top of everything from your body to the balls and the table conditions and yet it is relaxed awareness.

I can be in the Zen state without being "in the zone", and this is how I search for the zone and eventually find it. The wakefulness of Zen puts you in touch with yourself and the shots so that you can make the proper adjustments required to hone your shot-making system and get "in the zone", or just play really well consistently. There are different levels of the zone and the more Zen you are on a regular basis the more frequent and powerful the zone will be.

"The Zone" is a state of being where everything you do feels easy and almost effortless, yet it is an effort. You have mastered the "efforts" or the movements so well that you just slip into place on every shot and simplify what needs to be done, un-complicating the issue and alive with the peace of the moment because the way is open to you.

In pool, the more awake and observant you are while you practice, the faster you will improve because you are gaining valuable experience on every shot. Think of a happy baby who is just learning how to walk. Very wobbly yet very awake to what they are doing. If they stand up wrong and off-balance, they will fall down quickly. After falling on their behind several times, they learn to put more effort into standing up with balance or trying something different so they can keep their balance next time. Failure to learn how to walk is not an option for a baby.

To play Zen Pool you must be mindful on every shot so that finding a corrective course of action on the next shot or eventually in your session will be possible. Just have the attitude that figuring out the game is your only option. That is the Zen of improving at pool.

The Zen of playing pool at or near your capabilities (be it just under, right at, or above your skill level), is about being in touch in the moment with what you have figured out to work for you, and being present inside of that system. It also has something to do with getting warmed up and synchronizing your body, mind and spirit into the game. Give yourself a chance to let this happen.

Playing above your skill level or "over your head" is a good sign, as it means you are improving with the awareness you have placed into your dance through time. Embrace and expect this feeling. Always think that there is room for improvement as this will keep you awake.

When you are playing perfectly, pay attention to the level of awareness you are in and keep doing and noticing the same patterns of thought and movement as you go around the table. You can recall these moments in the future to elevate your play.

One night as a teenager when I was leaving my home to play in a local tournament my mother encouraged me by saying "Zen Pool Max, Zen Pool." I knew what she meant and it made me feel good. Although my mother Estelle has since passed away, while living she supported my pool playing in many ways and especially wanted me to just play like she knew I could.

The statement "Zen Pool" was a great gift from my mother as it is about so many profound elements of life and bringing those elements into playing pool. Just thinking of Zen brings you closer to that wavelength in your game and hence carries over into your life in general. In this sense, playing Zen Pool improves our lives away from the table as well as improving our game.

Zen Pool is playing for the love of the game, being in the moment, being aware of your body, paying attention, and having clear intentions. There is a Zen balance between letting go and holding on in what you are doing. Mental and physical awareness must be coupled with relaxation and calm of mind.

Playing for the love of the game enables you to play with focus for countess hours. When you are so excited about playing, it never gets old, partly because you are constantly learning new things in this Zen state. In the heat of pool battle, Zen will bring you right back to what is important in the now, making your shot and controlling the cue ball in the way you know best.

I invite you to make pool a form of meditation in which you discover the many beautiful and interesting facets of the game with your Zen awareness in the moment, and your Zen process of mastering yourself and the game.

Zen Pool
In Chinese Characters

TRUST
The Magic Ingredient

After all these years of playing pool, I have determined that the most important skill in the game is trust. Sure, fundamentals and knowledge are very important, but trust is the ingredient that gives life to concentrated effort.

If you do not know much about the game and have poor fundamentals, trust will not magically make your shots and put the cue ball into perfect position for you. So you will need to study the game and actively learn a sound way of playing pool. You will need to improve your skill.

Trust alone will not pocket the balls for you. You need craft, and this takes time and effort. Even if you have some good moments, you will need to keep working, keep learning and keep improving.

Trust is the final ingredient for a master of the craft. Trust is what makes champions play their best and light up a table. Trust is what enables a master to make the game look really easy. To a master who is clicking physically and mentally, the game is easy.

Yet trust is also the first ingredient to put you on the road to mastery. If you have a goal, a vision of how good you want to be, you have got to trust you will make it there before going down that road if you intend to succeed.

With this in mind, you have got to accept and expect that you will make mistakes on the way there, but trust that if you keep trying, you will correct those mistakes and move closer to your goal…closer every day. You have got to expect improvement.

It all boils down to the shot you are facing right now. On your very next shot, make a decision. Pick a contact point. Plan a position route. Decide on what spin to use. Decide how hard to hit the shot. And then when it is time to execute, try it and see what happens. Have desire to make it work, want it bad, and concentrate. But trust in your stroke. Put it out there. Let it go. Throw the cue. Relax. Let it happen.

Do not jump up on your shot. Do not clench the cue with a tight grip and give a half stroke. Do not try to steer the ball in the hole. Hey, if you do, you are only human, just do not do it forever. Calm down and trust your stroke.

If you have to, imitate a champion for a few minutes. Pretend you are that person. Walk like them, stroke like them, talk like them. This is actually one of the fastest ways to become great at something. Try imitating as many good players as you can. They are worthy of imitation; this will only help you.

Be an actor for a minute, and start acting like a great player. You just might become one. And if you are one, trust your stroke, trust your game.

Practice by yourself on a regular basis. Each time you practice, master one shot. Keep shooting it until you have it. If you keep making a change, you will have to get it right eventually. If you do this every day, that is a lot of shots in a year. Imagine if you mastered five shots a day. Trust the process and trust your stroke.

Here is the legend and fifteen-time World Champion Willie Mosconi in 1989 with your sixteen-year-old author. He was known as "Jumpin" Willie in his youth and "The White Heat" later on. Although no longer living, he still holds the official World Record continuous run without a miss in Straight Pool of 526 balls in Springfield, Ohio during an exhibition. (Unofficially, Babe Cranfield has a high run of over 600 balls. Babe's book, *The Straight Pool Bible*, is a must-have for any pool library.) The book *Willie's Game* is a great read about Mosconi, and his instructional books are classics that should be in every pool library.

My Grandfather Pop saw him play three times and each time he ran over 100 balls. Pop said, "There was nothing to watching him play because he made the game look so easy. If he wanted to draw the cue ball 6 inches, he drew it 6 inches; if he wanted to draw the cue ball 8 inches, he drew it 8 inches." These words from my grandfather about Willie's game inspired me to work extra hard on my cue ball control. You can imagine what a thrill it was for me to meet Willie Mosconi on that summer day. (Photo by your author's Mother Estelle.)

TWO FOCUSES ON EACH SHOT

Playing pool at the top level requires that you do two things on every shot: Pocket the object ball and control the cue ball. This requires a certain amount of discipline to accomplish this goal shot after shot. First of all, detailed mental planning is essential for you to achieve ideal results. At the very least, this means deciding where in the pocket you want the object ball to drop, and picking a small area for the cue ball to land (the smaller the better).

Once you start to acquire knowledge and skill in pocketing balls and playing position, it becomes a task to master doing both at the same time, during the same shot.

Of course, consistently pocketing balls is the first step. Beyond visual skill and talent, being able to form a stable bridge, and the aptitude to deliver a consistent stroke, keeping your body still is the major skill in the ball pocketing department.

You will see it in almost any amateur tournament: someone misses a ball while jumping up or moving their body much more than normal. Once a player masters sound fundamentals, visual skill in lining up once again becomes the most important factor.

Now, getting the cue ball to land where you want requires a lot of feel and the certainty that you will make the ball you are shooting at. If you are a precision planner, you will find that the cue ball usually lands on your target only when you do make the ball anyway.

Accurate cue ball positioning is based on accurate object ball pocketing. You will find that you can make a ball but miss position simply because you did not make the ball in the specific part of the pocket that your position route required, or you did not "cheat" the pocket properly.

For the most part though, you can run out by just making the balls in the center of the pocket opening or "pro side of the pocket," as long as you keep nice angles on your shots.

In a later article "Attack the Shot and Then Position" (page 49), I explain how you must secure the shot with your set up and then focus on touch to get position. This is true: However, at the moment your cue tip is contacting the cue ball, you must still be present fundamentally and visually to pocket the ball while you deliver your stroke. It is your internal sense that must be focused on controlling the cue ball.

A major key is to deliver your stroke like you "just know" the object ball is going in. Hitting a shot in this way will give you maximum feel for controlling the cue ball. Of course, you will "just know" the object ball is going in with a good set up, visual focus, and keeping your body still. So plan accurately, stay down, and shoot with confidence!

Be aware of the cue ball and the object ball at once. (Photo courtesy of Jeremy Wheat)

HOOP CONTROL

A very sharp student of mine recently informed me that more than two basketballs can fit in a regulation basketball hoop at the same time, and that good players actually aim for the ball to go into a certain part of the hoop depending on the situation. Maybe I should not have been surprised, but I was, and I earned an even greater respect for higher level basketball.

This same student of mine was excited when I told him about "cheating the pocket" and demonstrated to him that more than two pool balls can fit into a pocket at the same time, which is true on most tables. Even if two balls cannot fit in, there will still be some room to work with. "Cheating the pocket" is basically deciding what part of the pocket you want the object ball to enter, either to increase your chance at pocketing the ball or to change the cue ball's rebound angle off the object ball for playing position on the next shot. Professionals do this all the time. Because the pockets on most pool tables are pretty wide, this can lead to a little carelessness and slight loss of accuracy in shot-making. By just trying to make the ball into the pocket in general, it may bobble in a few times and even miss once in a while.

The forgivingness of the pockets may lead to carelessness. Sometimes I have caught myself playing worse on a big pocket table than I do on a tight pocket table. So what I do now is try to pretend I'm playing on a tight table and this helps me keep focused.

No matter how wide the pockets are, I like to make it a habit of picking an exact spot in the pocket as a target for the object ball. Picking this spot helps me find a clean line for the object ball and a clean contact point, which in turn helps me find a clean stroking line onto which I can balance my stance.

It is amazing how accurate you can be at hitting a certain part of the pocket, even when the object ball is several feet from the opening.

As long as there are no obstructing balls in the path, it is important that the spot I pick is in the "professional side of the pocket." The professional side of the pocket is the actual opening, as opposed to the entire visual entity of the pocket. See Diagram A. This will help you avoid hitting the rail on the way in, something that drove Willie Mosconi mad.

You will need to "Cheat the Pocket" to gain position quite often. The closer the object ball is to the pocket, the more lee way you will have to alter the angle at which the cue ball leaves, see Diagram B.

When the object ball is close to the pocket, your chances of missing are slim, but you will still need to be accurate for the purpose of controlling the cue ball.

When the object ball is a couple feet or more from the pocket, and you need to cheat the pocket to create more angle for the cue ball, your chances of missing are greater.

Yet if you always make it a habit to go for an exact spot in the pocket, even when you have a perfect angle, you will have more confidence and ability in cheating the pocket at a distance when you need to, see Diagram C.

When I do have a perfect angle on a shot, the spot I pick in the pocket will be right in the middle of the professional side of the pocket. If the object ball is near the rail, my spot will be on the pocket facing. If the ball is out in the open, my aiming spot will be in the middle or close to the middle of the pocket, on the rim of the slate.

Try practicing with pool balls on a snooker table for a few minutes if the room owner lets you. Then, when you go back to the pool table, you will see just how much room you have to play with. Have fun.

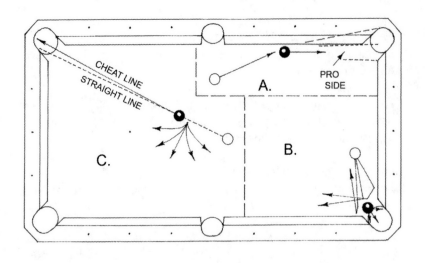

CHEAT LINE
STRAIGHT LINE

A.

PRO
SIDE

B.

C.

18

MINIMIZING CHAOS

A chaotic system is one that shows sensitivity to initial conditions. Any uncertainty in the initial state of the given system, no matter how small, will lead to rapidly growing errors in any effort to predict future behavior.

Basically, very small changes can result in greatly different final states in a weather system; this could mean that the flapping of a butterfly's wings in Australia may lead to the formation of a hurricane in the Caribbean; hence the "butterfly effect." In a pool shot or "system," this could mean that a slight change in the way you address the cue ball could entirely change the outcome of the shot.

If you watch a good pool player who first started out playing snooker, you may notice that he has exceptional ball pocketing skills. This is partly because snooker requires tremendous aiming accuracy to pocket a ball; however, excellent cueing skills are equally important.

Out of necessity, world-class snooker players are not only excellent at keeping their body still; they have finely honed a skill which surely comes in handy for playing all types of pool—ACCURATELY CUEING THE CUE BALL!

In saying "cueing the cue ball," I am referring to the contact point between the cue's tip and the cue ball at impact. Accurately cueing the cue ball means that the player actually hits the cue ball on the spot that he intended to strike. If a pool shot is the result of a chaotic system, then the behavior of the balls can be predicted only if the initial conditions are known to an infinite degree of accuracy, which is supposedly impossible. However, a pool shot does not unfold completely because the balls will eventually stop due to the friction of the cloth.

Now, imagine there was not any friction between the balls and the cloth and you had to accurately predict the exact route of a seven hundred and twenty five rail bank shot! Can you see how minor discrepancies in where you cue the ball and the speed with which you hit it can show up way down the line?

Have no fear, though, as under present conditions it is within the realm of possibility to predict and control those little colored balls with hair-raising accuracy. This does require concentration as the outcome is still very sensitive to initial conditions.

Cueing the cue ball and following through are like addressing a letter to a friend. Where you cue the cue ball will take it to the right zip code, and the speed will take it to the mail box for perfect position.

However, if you give an incorrect address, the cue ball and object ball(s) may arrive in the wrong state!

Increasing your awareness of where you are hitting the cue ball will definitely improve your position game. If you have the discipline to pay attention to this, you will also become a more consistent shot-maker by learning how minute differences in spin can affect deflection and your line of stroke. For more on deflection see the article "Allowing for Deflection" on page 67.

Next time you practice, try directing most of your consciousness towards cueing the cue ball. Even though you will be looking at the object ball on the last follow through, you can still be aware of the cue ball. With practice and good form it will become second nature.

One thing to try is looking at the cue ball on your final stroke once you are confident in your line of aim. This will force you to stay still and give you a new awareness of cueing the cue ball.

Also practice your center ball hit by putting the cue ball on the head spot (the spot on the end of the table where you break from), shooting it over the foot spot (the spot on which the front ball is racked) and having it rebound off the end rail so it comes straight back to hit your cue tip. This improves your awareness of center ball and thus your ability to put small increments of spin on the cue ball. Anywhere on the vertical-center ball axis is still a center ball hit, and it is good to practice center ball follow (top spin) and center ball draw (bottom spin) as well.

My grandfather Charles "Pop" Eberle was still running out into his later years. When he was 83, I got him to play me a few games after he had not played in months. He picked his cue off the rack and proceeded to break and run 3 straight racks of 9-Ball on the family's 9-foot Brunswick Commander! During the Great Depression, he drove across the U.S. hustling pool to send money back home to my grandmother Francis and their kids...they ate well.

LOCK AND LOAD

Finding the stroking line, setting up your feet, and developing and preparing your bridge hand for each shot all require attention before your stance is complete. What about the stroking arm though; doesn't that need preparation, too? Absolutely.

Your stroking arm is basically your weapon in pool and you need to prep it or position it before dropping into your stance. It is similar to a fighter positioning his arms and body right before throwing a punch.

First, the feet are positioned and stabilized, then the torso is turned and the punching arm is cocked back and ready to punch. In pool the feet are set, the torso turns and the stroking arm gets locked and ready to load into the stroking line, along with the prepped bridge.

I like to teach putting your grip, wrist, elbow and shoulder all on the stroking line for the ideal alignment. This allows your stroke to swing vertically back and forth from your elbow, which serves as a hinge.

Granted, as proven by the great players with sidearm or underarm strokes, a perfectly vertical alignment is not necessary; just ideal.

Those sidearm players still set up the same every time on the stroking line and have tremendous hand-eye coordination and lots of practice to keep the cue in a straight line. The side arm also serves them by keeping their stroke away from their body. This will be achieved with my recommendations. Plus, you will have the benefits of a vertical pendulum motion with your forearm.

The stroking line is actually within a vertical plane as well, and it is in this plane where the grip, wrist, elbow and shoulder of the stroking arm reside when they are in the textbook stance.

My main point here is to have you try and get all these components inside the vertical stroking plane before and as you bend down into your stance. Now, by the time you are down, you know your stroking machine is already dialed into the shot.

You can actually configure your arm into a plane at any time and then place that plane right into the stroking plane. So, just like making a bridge before placing it on the table, you can lock in your stroking arm before taking your stance. In time, your whole stroking arm drops into the stroking plane as one unit ready to fire.

Eventually, your form will blend into one entity with all the pieces working together in perfect unison. Until you get there, each piece will take plenty of work to develop and will most likely feel awkward or strange in the earliest stages. This is normal. It is like learning a language or learning to dance. You must learn the vocabulary and then how to put it all together, and with lots of practice it eventually all flows together with ease.

Now you can speak, dance, and play pool, right? Part of the fun is enjoying the learning process while knowing in your heart that you will get there with patience, persistence, and determination.

The stance setup begins while you are standing. Here, your author is looking at the stroking line with the components of his stroking arm already put into place and the body facing the same direction as it will be during the stance. Pulling your hip away from the cue makes it easy to keep your center of vision and stroking arm on the stroking line.

In order to achieve this position from the standing position, all that must be done is to step out with the left foot first and then move the body backwards while keeping the alignment with the arm and eyes. Notice your author's right shoulder, elbow, wrist and grip. All on a vertical plane which includes the cue (stroking line) and center of vision. Even though you cannot see any of the components of your right arm, you can develop the feel to know where they are, and place them where you want so they all work together as a machine. Practice a few racks one handed like this with your focus on shooting arm alignment. (Photo courtesy of Jeremy Wheat)

A KEY TO CONSISTENT SHOT-MAKING

While there is no single trick to consistently pocketing balls, there are a few of them that, when combined, make for a very nice equation. One extremely important element to this equation is body positioning, or what I call "lining up into the shot."

Have you ever been down on a ball ready to shoot when you suddenly had the feeling that you were not aiming on the proper line? The answer is yes, I would guess. If so, what did you do about it? Perhaps you made a correction by pivoting your torso slightly, bending your knees differently, moving your bridge hand, leaning over, or trying to steer your cue in a better direction on your last stroke.

If you often find yourself using one or more of the above elixirs, then at least you do have the desire to pocket balls, but probably feel that life could somehow be more rewarding.

By adjusting your body once you have already assumed your stance, you are losing accuracy by hindering other important parts of the shot-making equation. These include good balance, proper cueing of the ball, relaxation, ample preparation (warm up strokes, feeling, mental comfort), and a straight stroke from your center of vision to name a few.

Now, have you ever lined up on a shot feeling right, only to change your line of aim because of doubt, and then realize that you would have made it had you followed your first instinct? Imagine if you could utilize that keen instinct on every shot. With a little cultivating, you can. You have got to develop a sense of trust that you have already positioned your body correctly on every shot.

Practice making a commitment to the line of aim that you initially determine as being correct. Trust and commitment begin while you are standing upright. It is important to be deliberate in choosing where to stand on each shot and in crouching down into the line of aim.

Basically, it is best to position your body correctly into each shot so that you can properly execute the fundamentals. If you feel like you will miss, stand up and reposition your body. Also remember to allow for spin when you are lining up your body into the shot.

Try shooting a few racks like this: On each shot, put your focus on aiming and finding the angle while you are standing, and position your stance accordingly. Once you are in your stance, take one back swing and shoot the shot. You may even close your eyes after that first back swing. Feel free to smile when you hear balls dropping into pockets!

Your author finishes a stroke at the 2006 World 14.1 Championship. The body did not need to move because it was positioned in the right place from the very beginning of the stance. (Photo: www.onthehill.jp)

Lining up into the shot or body positioning; this is a major key, if not the major key, to consistency in pool. By the time the bridge hand is planted onto the table, the shot is basically made. It is important to be looking down the stroking line past the cue ball and towards the object ball as you shift from standing to the shooting stance.

Looking at the cue ball on your way down will give you no assurance that you will be properly lined up. Rather, look at the object ball (contact paint, ghost ball, or whatever you like to aim with) and see the cue ball in your peripheral vision as you descend into your stance. If you line up on the stroking line to begin with, the cue ball will be in the proper place when you are in your stance. Let your bridge arm fully extend so your bridge lands in place rather than putting it down early and sliding your bridge into place. (Photo courtesy of Jeremy Wheat)

THREADING THE NEEDLE

Have you ever tried to thread a needle? When you tried for the first time, did you notice that you could hold the thread steady *until* you approached the eye of the needle, and when it was almost there your hand shook and the thread missed the eye? Attempting to pour liquid into the mouth of a very small-necked bottle may often result in the same kind of shaky muscle behavior. You can hold your hand perfectly steady until you try to accomplish your purpose; then, for some strange reason, you quiver and shake and spill the liquid. In medical circles this is called "purpose tremor." It occurs in normal people when they try too hard, or are "too careful" not to make an error in accomplishing some purpose.

In playing pool, these purpose tremors may lead to a missed ball. It may occur in a pool player if he is being excessively careful or too anxious not to miss a shot. Excessive carefulness and anxiety both have to do with too much concern for possible failure, or doing the "wrong thing," and making too much of a conscious effort to do right.

You can avoid "dogging it" by training yourself to stop "trying" too hard or being overly-careful at the moment you deliver your stroke. You must learn to trust your stroke.

Do your best to position your body into the stance with your center of vision and cue stick on the stroking line, and have keen focus on the contact point before you begin your stroke. Now, with your body perfectly still, your eyes focused on the contact point and not a thought in your mind, freely swing your arm forward in a pendulum motion.

When you are first learning your stance, it will require much work just to get aligned properly for each shot, and may feel awkward. Yet the more you practice good form, the more natural it will become, and getting into your stance will also be like threading a needle.

You develop a trust that your body is lining up to what you are looking at, and with trust comes confidence. The trick is to keep your body still as you relaxingly and confidently throw the cue with your shooting arm.

So many times a dogged shot is accompanied by a sudden jarring of the body at the time of the forward stroke or a stroke that obviously deviates from its usual relaxed and straight path. Again, this often comes from being overly careful and anxious.

It may help to remind yourself to "trust your stroke" or that "I'm just going to move my arm" before you get down on a shot. Also, taking deep belly breaths to ease possible tension in your torso and to get more oxygen to your brain can be helpful.

Try hitting some long straight-ins and angled shots with your body perfectly still and your eyes glued to the contact point. Then move only your arm with no concern for the outcome, just detached observation to the feeling and results of the shot.

If you have a habit of moving your body on your stroke, you may not even notice it when you do move. Even if you have someone to alert you when you do move, try to develop that body awareness so you will know without someone telling you.

Even though you will be looking at the contact point on the object ball, you must focus on keeping still as you deliver your stroke with perfect trust.

Do not "try" to stroke straight, do not "try" to make the ball. Just swing your arm forward and keep your body still and see what happens. You may discover incredible powers to make difficult shots look easy, even in pressure situations.

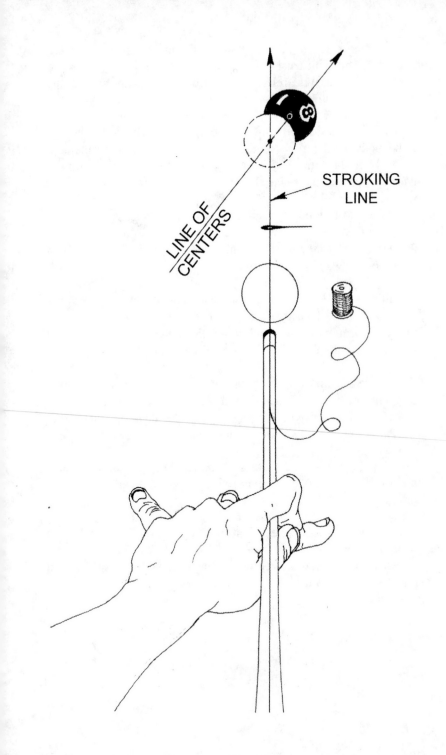

LINE OF
CENTERS

STROKING
LINE

Here is a photographic view of the stroking line taken from the author's perspective. (Photo courtesy of Jeremy Wheat)

TOTAL RECALL

Can you remember what it is like to be in *The Zone*? The ease with which you pocket balls and dance the cue ball into perfect position? The clarity with which you see all the right points, lines, angles and patterns? The inherent knowingness of the speed of the cloth and bounciness of the rails?

The experience of being a well-balanced and oiled pool-shooting machine, moving with infinite grace and delivering effortless smooth strokes that seem to fall off your backswing like so much snow falls off a leaf that can no longer carry the weight? The feeling of freedom and creativity in improvising and transcending perceived limitations?

Can you remember gliding around the table, radiant with confidence, completely absorbed in clicking colored balls over felt into pockets like a great surgeon performing intricate surgery?

When the only difference between deciding exactly where you want the cue ball and landing it there is the time in between? When the thought and the deed become one and the gap between willing and experiencing is closed? This, my friend, is *The Zone*. This is mastery. *The Zone* can be reached by you in your basement or in the U.S. Open finals on television in front of millions of people. Wherever you are, it feels great and fills you with a euphoric peacefulness that lifts you to a higher state of consciousness and increases your present moment awareness.

That's what it's all about, and when lots of people are watching, they get to go along for the ride. This is one reason Tiger Woods has such a tremendous following—through his concentration and mastery, fans are captivated and hopefully reminded of their own potential for mastery.

Sometimes *The Zone* can be elusive. Distractions in the form of thoughts or external stimuli can dilute our concentration and prevent us from finding that fanciful place. Do not, however, abandon ship just because the wind has disappeared. Keep your oars in the water and, before you know it, a powerful gust will come along to fill your sails.

Many times have I been playing awfully, only to be persistent and find myself in *The Zone*. Get focused, maybe you just needed to warm up.

If you want to be in *The Zone*, call it forth. Whatever your level, you have surely had "on" moments, and with good practice, they only get better and more frequent. Recall what it feels like, how you were moving, what you were thinking, what your eyes were doing, everything about it. Just pretend you are there and soon enough you will remember; you will be there.

Ken Demske awards your 22-year-old author the Champion's Plaque for the second straight year at the 1994 National Collegiate Championships put on by the ACU-I (The Association of College Unions International). (Photo courtesy of the ACU-I)

FROM LITTLE ACORNS DO MIGHTY OAKS GROW

In pool, as in life, it is the little things you do over and over that create the reality you experience, and it is your thoughts which control your actions. You do have the freedom to choose your thoughts at all times. You must be very clear about your desired results so that you can create thoughts, and hence action, that will produce the intended outcome.

When you are faced with a shot and have already determined where you want the cue ball and object ball(s) to go, then it is time to figure out the best way to get them there.

Now, formulate your approach considering the path of the balls, spin, speed, stroke, stance, bridge, equipment, humidity and so on. Next, imagine the shot happening perfectly in your mind. If you think you cannot do this, think again—you can.

Visualize the exact line and resting point of the cue ball instead of thinking "in that direction somewhere over there." While in games such as 9-Ball you can run out by playing area position, it will always improve your touch to pick an exact spot within the position zone.

See the line or gutter of the object ball going right into the pocket instead of "towards the pocket." You may be playing on tight pockets or have to squeeze the object ball around interfering balls. Many times it is necessary to shoot the ball into a certain side of the pocket for position's sake, so develop clarity of purpose. Do your best not to miss a shot on account of position.

Feel your cue tip strike the cue ball. Then, feel the cue ball roll, hit the object ball, slide, spin, jump, decelerate and stop as if you were one with the ball; because you are, feel the object ball roll and drop into the empty space.

My grandfather asked Willie Mosconi what was the most important thing in pool, and he said "touch." Hear the cue ball click the object ball, smack the back of the pocket, or softly drop in and roll into the ball return tray. Smell the dust swirling up from the pockets and taste what it feels like to sink a shot with perfect position, run a rack, or five, or a billion – it's up to you. What do you think?

Big runs do not happen in one shot, and yet they do. *Every* shot is *"The Shot."* Always keep your mind on the present shot, because that is *all there is*. So make the best of it and concentrate. Every shot is *your prayer to the universe*, but it does not really matter what you are doing. What you are being in relation to what you are doing makes all the difference.

So be positive, confident, focused, relaxed, determined. You name it; your game can only get better. If you consistently think clear, positive thoughts, you will consistently get clear, positive results. Feel free to discard negative thoughts at any time, and replace them with new ones; higher ones. If you should happen to miss, *big deal*! Be stubborn and keep your ideals. Create rhythm, remember who you are…and remember to breathe.

Hsin Huang of Taiwan is a talented player who has dominated the Northwest Women's Pool Association Tour (NWPA) and is one of the best players on the WPBA (Women's Professional Billiards Association). She has excellent technique which really helps her play so consistently. (Photo: Hsin Huang)

BRIDGE LANGUAGE

In pool, your bridge hand will determine how well you can communicate to the cue ball where it needs to go. Developing your stroke is also important, but now we will focus on the bridge hand, that device which guides the stroke and helps keep it on line.

Some people simply have more dexterity than others and quickly learn to form sound and solid open-hand and closed-hand bridges. For others, making a sound bridge comes in varying degrees of difficulty and the time spent in developing the bridge hand is especially well worth it.

All of our hands are unique, and if you do not have the bendy double-jointed fingers of many of the pros, just try to maximize the potential that your fingers give you. If you simply cannot make a good closed-hand bridge no matter how hard you try, you can still be effective with a good open hand bridge.

Think of someone fluent in sign language. They easily change from one distinct symbol to the next as they communicate. When they transform from one symbol to the next, do they fidget with their fingers for a while as they form the next symbol? Not if they are fluent.

That is the idea with pool. It is ideal to be able to smoothly and easily lock your bridge hand into the chosen form for the present shot. Many top players will even form their bridge in the air and finalize it by squishing it onto the table, thus locking it in place right away.

Locking your bridge in ASAP will enable you to focus on your stroke and speed control, instead of diverting your attention between getting your bridge hand ready and preparing your stroke. This is chasing two birds with one stone if you will.

My friends tease me for forming bridge hands all the time when I am away from the table. I used to do this in school and use my pencil as a pool cue while perfecting my bridges. So this is one way to practice and improve your game, work on your bridge while driving (keep one hand on the wheel please), watching TV, etc... Because there are many bridges in pool, you can work on any of them at any time. What can I say, I am a pool nut.

Try not to keep moving your bridge fingers around once you are in your stance. Learn to get them into place right away and put enough pressure into the table to keep them locked there even and especially on your final delivery.

The more fluent you become with your bridge hand, the more accurate and consistent you will also become.

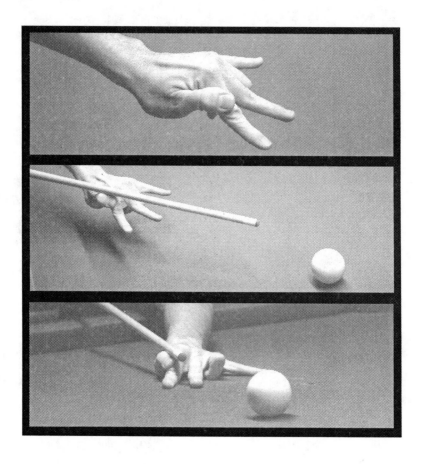

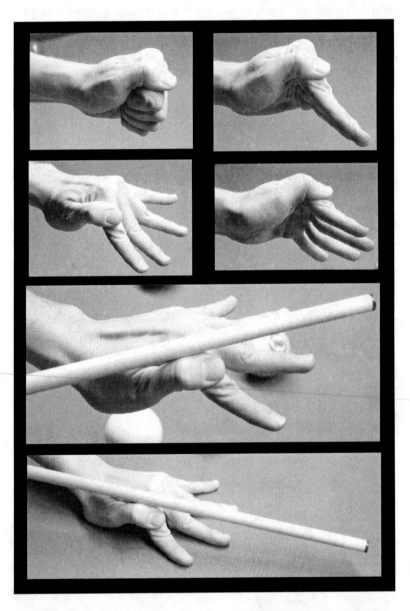

The photos up top are to aid you in forming a solid open-hand bridge. Notice how the bridge is fully-formed in the air with the cue in the groove on top of the thumb. When you plant your open hand bridge on the table, put the entire heel of the hand on the table for most shots. (Photos courtesy of Jeremy Wheat)

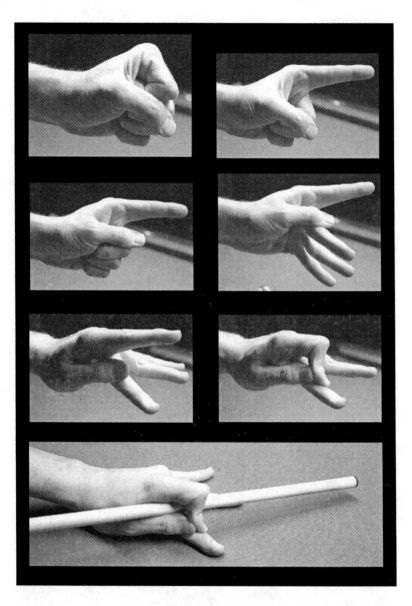

Step-by-step on how to form a closed-hand bridge. Begin at the top and go from left to right. (Photos courtesy of Jeremy Wheat)

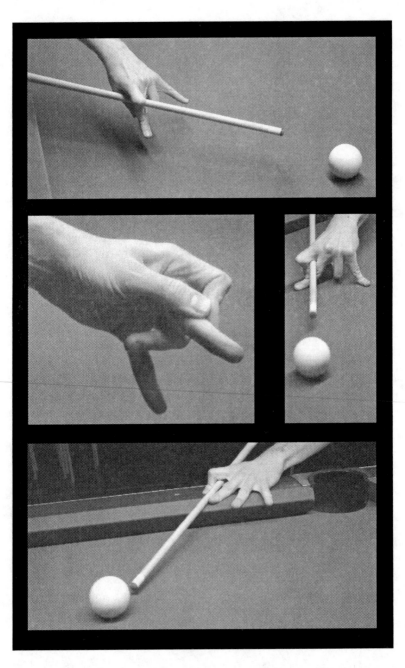

More bridge photos for you. (Photos courtesy of Jeremy Wheat)

COME BACK STRONG

It would be nice to jump out to an early lead and cruise to an easy win in every match you play. Everything goes your way while your confidence soars and you play perfect pool, cruising with your beautiful performance to another textbook win. The perfect pool dream situation every time you step up to play.

While this would be nice and sometimes does happen, the reality is that it does not always happen, and if you are unprepared for something less than your great expectations, your performance and your winning percentage will surely drop.

Sometimes it is adversity that pushes us to peak performance and to realize this is a blessed thing in this game.

So often, without wrongdoing on your part, you can and will find your self trailing in a match to varying degrees. And sometimes one or two little errors or bad rolls will put you behind in a match. Or maybe all the rolls went against you and you played miserably. The point is that there are countless ways to fall behind, and the more tournaments you play, the more of these ways you will experience.

So while you must try hard to make things go your way, you must be prepared for when they do not, and have the necessary mental and physical ammunition by your side to turn things around. For one, many players lose their edge once they have you down because they get comfortable and start to take winning for granted. Then when you fire back, they are caught off guard and falter. The heat is on them when you start coming back. Knowing this should be enough to make you keep bearing down.

Also realize that if they do not win any more games, they cannot win. Come up with the score you must beat them by from that point to win. If they are up 6-2 in a race to 9, then you have to beat them at least 7-2 from there out. That gives you a goal and a positive mind frame.

Nick Varner, the most legendary come-from-behind player of all time, told me, "I just always like to try one hundred percent on every shot." Thanks, Nick. That thought has won me countless matches. I often feel like I'm still the favorite to win the match, even when I'm trailing in the score.

So do not bitch, whine, complain, or feel sorry for yourself if things do not look great—get out there and play, try your best, give 100%. Many times that is the only way out, and many times you will make it out!

Physically keep a winning posture and keep breathing deeply from your belly. This will keep oxygen in your brain, and the winning posture will give you and your opponent the message that you are a champion and will not go away! It's never over until the last ball drops.

Jasmine Ouschan of Austria, winner of the 2006 BCA Open 9-Ball Championships Women's Division. In 2006 she made the quarter finals of the mostly men's World Straight Pool Championship, and the final 16 in 2007. If or when a woman is going to win a major men's pro event, she is certainly a top contender for such an achievement. Here you can see her determination; exactly what it takes to make great comebacks. (Photo courtesy of Rick Schmitz and azbilliards.com)

CUE BALL COMPASS

In all pool games, accurate direction control is essential for playing great position. While speed is also crucial, you must first get the cue ball traveling towards your target. With a nice medium angle, you can pretty much get the cue ball to go anywhere you want on the table.

Sometimes you can get away with being a little less accurate with direction control because the position zone is so big, but other times being off by one degree can mess up a run.

As a rule, I'm always going for an exact line with my cue ball. Even if I don't get the ball perfectly on that line, it will be closer than if I did not pick that line. The same goes for position play. I'm always trying to land the cue ball on an exact spot. By choosing an exact spot for my cue ball to land, it enables me to choose an exact direction for the cue ball to get there.

Practicing your direction control will be very beneficial to your game. Just choose a shot and keep setting it up exactly the same every time but work on getting the cue ball to travel on a different line after it pockets the ball.

Once you get the cue ball to go on your desired line, just pick a new line to work on.

The diamonds are good to use as targets. When you get good at hitting all the diamonds, your brain will fill in the rest and you will be able to hit any intermediate target line you choose during a game.

I would also recommend combining speed control with this drill just to keep you in the habit of hitting each shot with an intended speed. Practice like this will pay huge dividends.

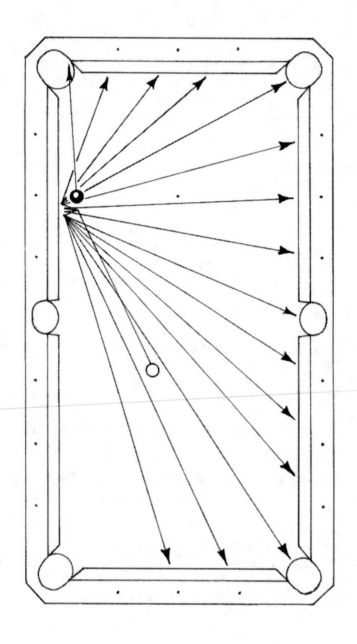

NEED FOR SPEED

My philosophy on playing position is that if you always go for an exact target on the table (the size of a dime to a cue ball), you will be in line much more often than not, and when the time comes when you have to play tight position, you will be ready.

By going for an exact target, you will also improve very fast because on every shot you are learning a nuance about cue ball control, even when you don't land on your chosen spot. Each "unsuccessful" attempt is showing you a way not to shoot the shot, thus increasing your knowledge and skill. So be encouraged if you miss the target—you are getting better!

In the last article, "Cue ball Compass," I discussed the importance of direction control in position play. The other half of the equation is speed control. Now that you can get the cue ball to go in the right direction, you need to make it land at your desired distance.

When you have a long *line of position* that gives you a good shot for the next ball anywhere along its length (usually towards or away from the next ball), speed control is not as urgent as when the cue ball must cut across such a line and into a small position zone.

If you always go for a specific spot even when you send the cue ball down a long *line of position* (have a big position zone), you will become better able to achieve position when you absolutely must be precise with your speed. Your cue ball speed control will become well-honed from always choosing a spot; even when not required.

I think developing excellent speed control is a matter of setting high standards for your position play and working to hone your touch. If you have the discipline to pick the spot for the cue ball, even on easy shots where the position zone is large, your game will advance by leaps and bounds.

I recommend setting up a shot, picking a target for the cue ball, and shooting it until you land exactly on that spot. Just by successfully executing this one shot, your speed control will improve for all the other shots on the table. Set up as many position scenarios to work on as you like; it will only help.

I also like to work on both my follow (top spin) and draw (bottom spin) speeds by mastering several different distances. As with working on direction control, your brain will fill in the gaps and you will soon be able to hit any intermediate target you wish, or at least get close enough for great shape. Just feel the speed, and trust that you will land the cue ball on your target.

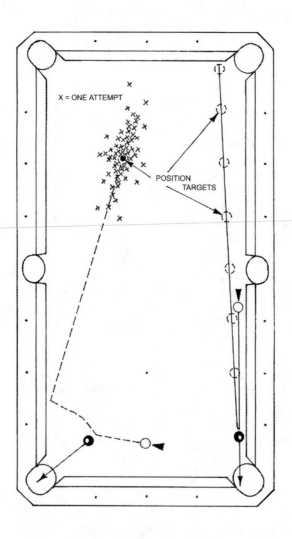

ATTACK THE SHOT...
AND THEN POSITION

Most successful pool shots consist of two parts; pocketing the object ball and positioning the cue ball. These two facets of each shot are so interrelated that it is hard to say one is more important than the other.

Of course, if you don't pocket the ball, position will not do you much good. And if you don't play position, you will have to be an escape artist to clear the table. Yet if you follow this advice you may find yourself pocketing more balls anyway, and having easier runs. Sound good?

What I mean by attacking the shot is to really focus on making the ball by setting up your stance so your cue is securely on the stroking line *before* you take your first practice stroke.

Remember, the stroking line is the line you will decide to actually throw (stroke) your cue down once you make all the necessary adjustments for speed angle and spin. It is ideal to decide on a line before you take your stance, because without this decision a proper stance and stroke are not likely to happen.

So in order to pocket the object ball, you must first know what you will be doing with the cue ball because this information could change the line you stroke down.

A major part of being secure on the stroking line is having your bridge fully formed and solid. Taking the time during your practice strokes to solidify your bridge will not only make your shot making weaker, it will also take valuable time away from prepping your stroke and getting the feel for moving the cue ball to its next location.

So get your bridge as ready as possible while you are bending down into the shot and try to snug your bridge into the table right away with the cue on the stroking line, of course.

Also be conscious of your grip hand so that while you take your stance and once you are down, the cue is right on the stroking line.

Equally or more important than your hands are your eyes. They actually come first, and should be on the stroking line while you are standing and all the way into your fully set stance. This is "hands-eye coordination." See the stroking line with your eyes and place the cue there with your hands. If this is not clean, your shots will not be clean.

So now that you have "attacked" the shot by aggressively setting up on the stroking line, you can shift your focus to feeling the speed of the shot and delivering a beautiful stroke. In my opinion, that's what the practice strokes are really for; feeling the position.

Of course you will be maintaining your aim and double checking where you will hit the cue ball, but the critical part of the shot-making process has already been attacked, and now you are feeling your cue ball out of a solid stance, bridge, and accurate cue ball/object ball collision. First, secure the shot by making a stance that is on line and solid before the first practice stroke, and then maintain it during your practice strokes and final stroke while you attack the exact position you desire.

Ga Young Kim of Seoul, Korea is the 2005 Women's World Champion and 2005 US Open Women's Champion. In true Zen style, she is very aware and focused in the present moment. Ga Young has big talent and plays her game with a lot of confidence. (Photo by Diana Hoppe)

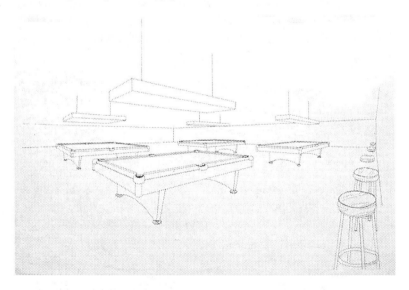

A two-point perspective drawing by the author while attending Washington & Lee High School in Arlington, Virginia, class of 1990.

MAKING COMBINATIONS

How many times have you heard another pool player say "I hate combinations!"? I've heard it a million times, and even from some true champions. This just shows how difficult combos can be, even for a good player.

Of course the difficulty level of combination shots varies greatly, but there are some things you can do to increase your success rate and you'll be surprised at just how many tough combos you will end up making.

Most of the time, it is wise to avoid most combos unless they lay easy or seem to be your only option. Having the control to work around combos is great, yet eventually you will need to make one and it is better to shoot it with confidence.

The first step for success, as usual, is mental. Learn to get rid of the "I hate combinations" attitude and dreadful self talk. Enter into the deal with positive anticipation and even tell yourself something like "I love making combinations!" Trust me, a positive attitude like this will at minimum double your combo success rate immediately! Condition yourself to think how much you enjoy making combos.

The accuracy required for making a combo means that you should take extra care in studying the shot and finding the contact points. Making a combination is very similar to making one object ball into a very small pocket.

While aim is important, I don't think the trick to making combos is in a special aiming technique. Rather, it is in using your technique well; and in being decisive and accurate in your delivery. Once you figure out your exact contact point and stroking line, you will need to zero in on it pretty quickly before it disappears to your eyes.

With a positive mind frame, your first step is to find the contact point on the ball you want to pocket. Do this carefully and pick a spot in the middle of the opening (pro side of the pocket). Now line up behind the ball you will be striking and carefully figure out where you need to hit this one with the cue ball. It is at this stage that I recommend you get your grip arm into alignment, and then place this arm at the angle to your body that it will be at during your shot. This will save you valuable seconds, and enable you to better lock in on the stroking line and contact point while they are fresh in your sights. Prepping your stroking arm will also give you much needed confidence as you head to the final stage of making the combo.

Everything you need to do well for shot-making, you need to do better for making combos, ha-ha! It is important that you are decisive as you line up into your stance. There is no room for wiggling around to get comfortable and find your aim. Aim should be neat and tidy, and you should decisively set your stance and get ready to confidently deliver your stroke. Because your aiming and preparation were so good, now all you have to do is stroke your cue down the groove that you have set yourself on.

Focus on a straight, smooth backswing and a straight smooth follow through…that's it. Do not think about making a combo, and do not jump up and try to steer the shot. Trust your process and focus on a clean delivery.

One great aiming technique for combos is using two ghost balls; one for the object ball to be pocketed and the other for the object ball you will be striking with the cue ball. Depending on how good you are at visualizing ghost balls, this will put you right where you need to be to make the combo. Now just trust it and fire away!

I like to take this one step further and see the two ghost spots (see the diagram on page 52 and the diagrams on pages 60 & 99 for help with the ghost spot). The ghost spot on the ball to be pocketed helps me find the ghost spot for the middle ball which I then use for my stroking line. This is so good that I really should not be telling you this, ha-ha.

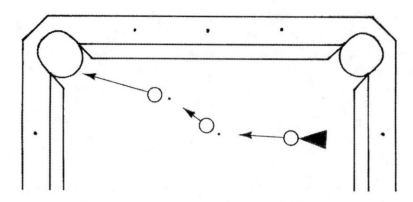

First, find the "Ghost Spot" for the object ball to be pocketed. Then, line up the middle ball toward that "Ghost Spot," to find the "Ghost Spot" that you will stroke the cue ball toward to make the combination. The ball in the middle will act as a cue ball and drive the final ball into the pocket. Remember, the "Ghost Spot" is $1\frac{1}{8}$-inch back from the edge of an object ball (because a regulation pool ball is $2\frac{1}{4}$ inches in diameter) and in line with the trajectory of the object ball being struck.

Your author stalks a game-winning combination on the 9-Ball on table twenty at Hollywood Billiards in Los Angeles, California. (Photo: courtesy of Charles Pinkett.)

FEEL THE FORCE

A good friend of mine at Hollywood Billiards recently asked me for some help with his pool game. After watching him closely for five minutes, I could see that he was tensing and kind of jumping up a bit on many of his shots. In addition, he was turning his stroke to either side as if trying to steer the ball into the hole.

I came up with a suggestion. I told him to line up for his shot, take a couple practice strokes, and to close his eyes right before and during his shot. That's right, I told him to close his eyes. He looked at me kind of funny but decided to give it a try. He missed the first shot or two, but then he started making just about everything he shot at, even long angled shots. Now he looked at me as if to say, "WOW! Unbelievable, I just made those shots with my eyes closed!" Even I was impressed with the shots he was making.

There are a few lessons to the story. One is: if you can just learn to stay out of your own way, you will be surprised at how accurate you really are. By jumping up or fidgeting on your delivery stroke, you are destroying the setup and aim you worked so hard to build. Second: shooting with your eyes closed proves just how important setting up is to your shot. If you do it well, you can literally shoot with your eyes closed! Third: if you work on your stroke, you can deliver it with your sense of feel and "muscle memory" once you get it lined up to your target. Closing your eyes will put your focus completely on what *you* are doing; not on whether you are worried about the ball going in or not.

When my friend closed his eyes, he no longer jumped or turned his cue during the stroke. It may take him a little time to bring that same calm in to his open-eyed game, but with some work he will do it.

While you practice with your eyes closed, pay attention to how your body feels during your shots and what parts move. Then, when you open your eyes again, remember the feeling and shoot as if your eyes are closed.

Practice a little with your eyes closed everyday for a week. This will improve your stance setup, help you keep your head and body still, and improve your feel for the game. Have fun practicing and may the FORCE be with you!

Efren "Bata" Reyes has put a spell on many audiences around the globe. Also known as "The Magician," he is considered by many international fans and players alike to be the best pool player of all time. He has won World Titles in 8-Ball, 9-Ball and One-Pocket and has an uncanny ability to win the big tournaments that pay between $100,000 and $500,000 for first place. The first time I went to the Philippines, he treated me to my birthday dinner with some friends and invited me to one of his favorite pool halls where he put on a dazzling display of 15-ball rotation (his specialty) in his flip-flops, while the children outside filled the windows to look in and catch a glimpse of the living legend in action. (Photo courtesy of azbilliards.com)

EYE SEE, EYE SEE!

It is essential to develop and maintain a consistent pattern of eye movement if you want to be consistently successful at the pool table. Your system should be focused and deliberate for maximum accuracy, efficient enough to help maintain rhythm, and relaxed enough to prevent confusion.

As a general rule for your practice strokes, look at the cue ball as you stroke toward it and until your cue stops near it, and look at the contact point on the object ball through and until the end of your back swing. Within your routine, you may choose to look at either the cue ball or object ball for one or more strokes in order to really key in on your accuracy. The reason you look at the cue ball when your tip is extended, is to prepare for the accurate cueing of the ball. That is also why you stroke directly towards the exact spot you want to strike. Remember, it is like a dress rehearsal for your stroke, so pay attention.

The reason to look at the object ball when you start your practice back swings is partially to keep your stroke on line (see article on page 87). You also need ample time to focus on the contact point (which is what I suggest looking at on 99% of your shots, however it is possible to look at the cue ball last) before you strike the cue ball. On your practice strokes you are verifying the contact point and making sure you are lined up to hit it. You are also verifying the stroking line and making sure your aim looks correct.

Now, it is up to you to put these ingredients together in a way that suits your own style; in particular, the number and speed of your strokes. It might be a good idea watch closely and learn from top players' eye patterns. Once you develop a system that works for you, be sure to use it in all situations. Sometimes the pressure of a match may disrupt your eye pattern and throw you off a bit. Try to get back into your pattern as soon as possible. Your eyes are amazing instruments and they will let you know if everything is on line—try using them in coordination with your cue stick.

FROM THE GROUND UP

As in any other active sport, playing pool requires the coordination of the entire body. While on most shots only the shooting arm moves, every part of the body is first placed in a specific location to allow the player to deliver an effective stroke for each shot.

While it may seem obvious, the feet must be placed correctly first in order for everything else to fall into place. While most of the action is on the table, it is the feet (or the wheels for the wheelchair players) that set up the action in the first place and stabilize it during the practice strokes and final delivery.

Just by watching closely, you will notice a multitude of foot positions assumed by different players. Each player develops or falls into a consistent way of positioning their feet for almost every shot.

I have noticed that beginners struggling with pool struggle to varying degrees with getting their feet set. They may line up initially only to shuffle their feet around once they are down there in search of being ready to shoot.

The reason why finding the stroking line before getting into the stance is so important, is that your foot positioning is determined by the location of the stroking line. And it is your feet that will set up the rest of your stance.

The more attention you pay to your foot positioning, the more success you will have on the pool table. Great players in all cue sports have put considerable time and effort into perfecting their foot positioning. They have worked hard for something that they now make look so easy and effortless. And sometimes even great players will work hard to reconfigure their foot positioning if they think it will take them to a higher level.

As proven by the fact that different champions have slightly different foot positions, there is no one "correct" position for your feet. Effective foot positioning will have attributes in common, such as: Allowing you to be *well-balanced* in your stance, allowing your stroking arm to be *free from the interference of your torso*, and providing you with *stability* for your stroke.

My basic recommendations for accomplishing these three objectives are: put the center of your *back* foot directly under your cue and on the stroking line, and your *front* foot away from the stroking line in the 30-60 degree angle range (although you can experiment outside of this range), pointed more forward than the back foot, and slightly more than shoulder width apart from your back foot (see diagram on page 58).

Foot positioning on specialty shots such as the break and jack up shots may be slightly different but they will still produce the three elements of balance, freedom, and stability.

You may often see a good player *first set his or her feet*, continue to stand upright for a moment, and then bend down to place their bridge hand on the table to complete the stance (this is what I want you to try). They may even bring their bridge and body partially or all the way back up for fine tuning, but while keeping their feet in place. Or they may stand up and reposition their feet again until they are comfortable. When a player is playing sharp and confidently, usually you will not see them readjust their upper bodies after their feet are set. Yet go ahead and do this if you need to in order to be comfortable.

While I like to teach that a great pool stance is a solid tripod created by your two feet (legs) and your bridge hand (arm), I think the existence of great one-handed players proves that it can be done with a bipod (just your feet & legs), and that the feet are of paramount importance.

While it is fair to say that the greatest one-handed player will probably never consistently beat the greatest two-handed player, I have heard incredible stories about what one handed players (not using a bridge hand) have accomplished.

If you practice getting your feet set before bending down to place your bridge hand, you will find yourself playing more consistently and reaching higher levels of play all the time. Enjoy the fruits of balance, freedom, and stability.

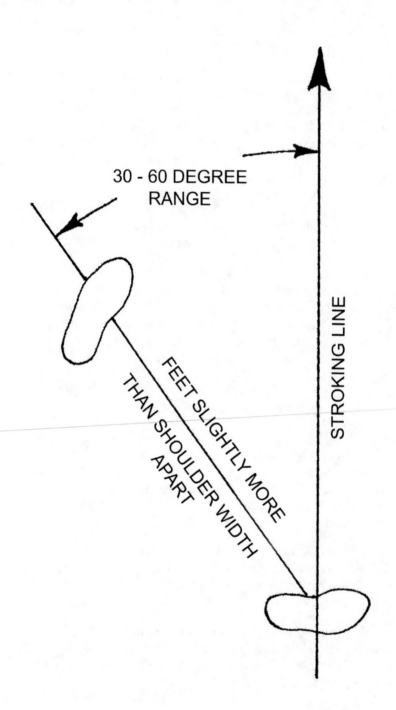

30 - 60 DEGREE RANGE

STROKING LINE

FEET SLIGHTLY MORE THAN SHOULDER WIDTH APART

TANGENT TIME

You know about the tangent line, right? For those of you who do not, it is the line perpendicular to the line that the object ball will travel down and into the pocket. This tangent line is on the contact point and leaves at a right angle from the collision (see the diagram on page 60).

The cue ball will travel along this line after impact and stay on this line if it came in from an angle, assuming there is no top or bottom spin on the cue ball. This knowledge is paramount in controlling the cue ball, so how will it help you to pocket your object ball?

This harkens back to a previous article on body positioning on page 25. It is to your advantage to position your eyes and cue stick correctly onto the stroking line from the standing position in order to obtain accuracy and consistency.

Now, look at the line from the object ball to the pocket.

Next, assuming there is an angle, imagine the tangent line coming off of the object ball from the contact point.

Now, with this right angle, or ∟, in mind, bend into the shot with the goal of caroming the cue ball off of the object ball and down that tangent line. If you can do this, the object ball will automatically drop.

You can extend this line to a rail and try to hit that spot, or you can extend it beyond the table to the wall or something, and go for that. Doing this will open your mind to the entire geometry of the shot. For a moment, taking away your focus from making the object ball and putting your focus on making the cue ball travel down the tangent line may help you deliver a smoother more relaxed stroke. This method may greatly increase your feeling for the game of pool!

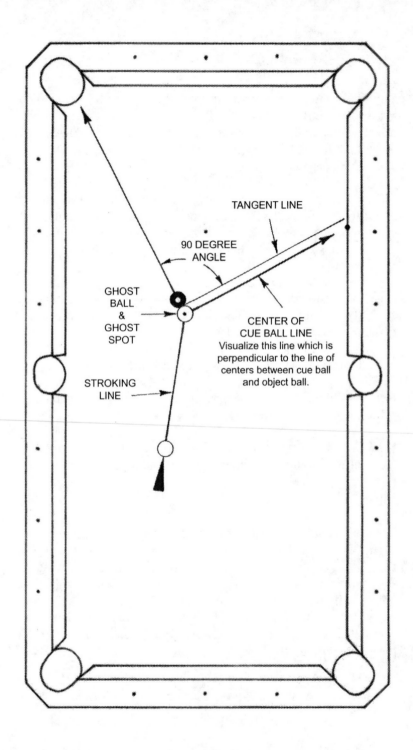

TANGENT LINE

90 DEGREE
ANGLE

GHOST
BALL
&
GHOST
SPOT

CENTER OF
CUE BALL LINE
Visualize this line which is
perpendicular to the line of
centers between cue ball
and object ball.

STROKING
LINE

Here is Manny "PacMan" Pacquiao, the superstar boxing champion from the Philippines, and your author at the Wild Card Boxing Gym in Hollywood, CA. Trained by legendary boxing trainer Freddie Roach, Manny is widely considered to be pound-for-pound the best boxer in the world today. Manny is also an excellent pool player capable of running many racks, and when he is in Manila there is no shortage of exciting pool action. In the Philippines, he has a platinum-selling album on which he sings and plays guitar, has his own event promotion company MP Productions, and is now entering politics to help improve the lives of his people. Manny sponsored your author to play in the 2006 World Pool Championship which was hosted at the PICC (Philippine International Convention Center) in Manila. (Photo courtesy of Wild Card Boxing Gym)

KEEPING YOUR COMPOSURE

Webster's Dictionary defines composure as "calmness; self-possession." (Webster's New World Dictionary, 2nd ed., Simon & Shuster, 1979, p. 101)

- Composure is remaining calm and focused enough to perform up to your capabilities.

- Composure is consistently responding to stressful situations with empowering thoughts, feelings and actions.

- Composure is letting go of past mistakes and breathing out anxieties about the future.

- Composure is laughing in the face of seemingly gargantuan pressure and concentrating on the task at hand.

Why would you want to have composure? Maybe you want to make great comebacks; or just play your game against a top player; or be a champion; or impress a potential significant other (show off). Whatever your reason, composure is a good place to start when you are striving for positive results.

It is similar to approaching life from a well-balanced center. If you do your best to keep balanced, you will have a better chance at staying afloat if something rocks your boat.

Gaining composure could mean changing the way you think about certain aspects of the game. I am sure you know a few players who go berserk every time their opponent gets a good roll. The more bad rolls they get, the more they freak out and start announcing to the world that you are lucky. Meanwhile, they are stuck in the past with a dark storm cloud growing over their head.

Granted, there is too much luck in nine-ball, but until the rules are changed to call all shots and safeties, it is necessary to understand that rolls happen and you should be happy to be at the table. If you find yourself on the short end of the rolls during a match, just think to yourself "things will turn my way," and do the best with what you have.

For example, what if you were on the hill with a seven game lead and your opponent comes back to tie the match? You could be in shell shock and flub a possible chance at a win, or you could understand that many matches are close anyway, and all you have to do is concentrate on each shot in this final game.

When you have a big lead it is especially important to bear down even more, and realize that if you go to sleep you have no chance at winning. No lead is a safe lead.

The same thing applies when you are coming from behind. No lead is insurmountable. Just think "I'll hold him there and then pass him." It is amazing to see what happens when you are unflappable. The more you understand match dynamics, the less likely you will be taken by surprise, and the more you will be giving the surprise.

Composure has a lot to do with knowing and remembering the truth about yourself and any given situation. Whether the heat is on or off, it is good to remember what you are capable of (physically, mentally, and spiritually) and let this give you confidence. Letting go of fears and doubts is one of the main challenges every pool player or and person in life for that matter must face.

The illusions of fear and doubt have no power unless you have allowed them the power. Once you learn to recognize illusions, it will be easier to get rid of them.

If the truth is that you play at a certain level, then you want to do your best to prevent anything from interfering. Often, blockages are very subtle and it would be wise to take a deep honest look into the causes. Once you have targeted any interference, it is necessary to actively and willfully diminish it by turning its positive counterpart into a habit. Sometimes habits die hard, but in the business of uncovering the truth it will be worth it.

If you are often too tense, learn to relax. If you are doubtful, learn to generate feelings of courage and confidence. If you have trouble concentrating, turn pool into a study on concentrating. Whatever the malady, there is a remedy, and a little discipline can go a long way.

Not enough can be said about the benefits of preparation. Before a big match, tell yourself that this will take everything you have, and that you must go deep to your basic core where your strength lies. If perhaps you have never beaten this player, tell yourself "that was then; this is now," or "I am due for a win."

Michael Jordan says that before he shoots a big foul shot, instead of thinking about the millions of people watching and everything at stake, he puts himself in a familiar place like his old high school gym where he feels comfortable.

Being physically and spiritually fit are also great bonuses. The link between your body language and your mental/emotional states is amazingly close. It is good to work just as hard on your composure (mental game) as you do on your physical skills.

Talk to experienced players and champions about this and read plenty of books like *Pleasures of Small Motions* by Bob Fancher, Phd., *Golf is not a Game of Perfect* by Bob Rotella, *The Inner Game of Tennis* by Timothy Gallway, and *Conversations with God* by Neale Donald Walsh.

CALM YOUR NERVES WITH FUN

I think we have all been there: played below our capability in a match because we were anxious, tight, or nervous for whatever reason. It is easy to make a huge deal out of a match even if it really does not mean much.

And it is easy to place all our focus on the outcome or anticipated outcome before it even happens. These thoughts about winning and losing, the other player, the crowd—all take away focus and hinder a relaxed state that is ideal for us to perform at our best.

Did you fall in love with pool because it gave you a chance to win at something? Or did you fall in love with pool because it is simply interesting and fun? Probably because it was so fun, right? And do you play your best when you are relaxed or when you are tense? I'm guessing when you are relaxed. I think having fun helps you to relax. Your heart rate is slower and your confidence often is higher. If you can have fun and concentrate, your stroke will be smooth and you will stay down on the ball better.

Next time you are nervous, tight, or worried before a match, remember you are about to go play some pool. It is not some test you must pass in order to preserve your life; it is a game of pool. Remind yourself of this before the match. Accept your nervous feelings and tell yourself that you will be getting calmer and calmer. Settle down. Really focus on setting your stance up where it needs to be, so you can have a relaxed stroke and focus on the speed control.

If you are sloppy with your setup and stance, you will be more likely to jump up when it is time to shoot. It is hard to control the cue ball if you don't feel the object ball will be dropping. While you don't want to have a sloppy setup, you also do not want to be too tight in your setup. Relaxed concentration is the key. You are relaxed and focused when you are in the zone.

Relax in between shots, too. Don't be so worried. Walk around like you know what you are doing. Look at Jose Parica in between his shots. It looks like he is taking a stroll in the park.

So many times the first game or two can set the emotional tone for the rest of the match. Many times your nerves will be calmed if you can do well in the beginning. Do not let your guard down, though, if things start out well, because one mistake in this sport can cost the whole match. So keep concentrating one shot at a time. Relax, and remember to have fun!

Jose "Amang" Parica is one of the greatest players of all time. Tournament director Scott Smith calls him "The Leader of the Invasion" because he was the first great Filipino player to arrive in the States. Jose has a famous ability to be relaxed and concentrate at the same time. Another one of his nicknames is "The Little Man with the Big Heart." Jose was a Golden Gloves Boxer in his youth. It pays to be tough in this game. (Photo courtesy of Bruce Clayton & azbilliards.com)

ALLOWING FOR DEFLECTION

One of the most time consuming things to master in pool is how to adjust your aim when using sidespin. While throw may exist between the cue ball and object ball, deflection has a much bigger impact on your aim for most shots.

My definition of deflection is: "When using left or right English, the tendency of the cue ball to deviate from the stroking line to the opposite side of that which you strike the cue ball. In addition, deflection increases with an increase in speed of stroke and with an increase in amount of sidespin."

With this definition in mind, making a pool ball while using side spin is no easy chore. Without this awareness, a player can never advance to the highest levels of play.

So, when and how much do you compensate your aim for the side spin you plan to use? The answer to the first question, when, is while you are standing before setting up your stance.

Since allowing for deflection will create a stroking line other than that of a center ball or vertical axis hit, you must decide on this line before getting down so you can create a stance that is balanced and aligned on this new stroking line.

The answer of how to find this new line is a bit more complicated. First of all, since you will be using sidespin, you will want to line your center of vision up through the side of the cue ball you will be striking (see diagram on page 69).

Do not simply stroke on a parallel line to that of a perfect center ball hit. Instead, you will have to pivot this stroking line away from parallel to the center ball hit line, in the direction of the cue ball side you will be striking (remember to do this while standing so you can get balanced on this line in your stance).

If there were no such thing as deflection, you could always stroke on a line parallel to the center ball stroking line when using English.

The less deflection a cue has, the less you will have to pivot your stroking line to make the shot.

Determining how much to pivot this stroking line requires experimental, repetitious and methodical practice for however long it takes to "get it." Good old fashioned blood, sweat and tears.

I suggest setting up the exact same shot over and over. Hit the shot with the same spin and speed while only adjusting your line of aim. By keeping the other variables the same you will quickly learn how much to pivot on that particular shot.

Then see what happens when you keep your spin and aim the same, but change your speed. Then keep your speed and aim the same while adjusting your spin.

Closely observe your results every shot so you can learn what is happening. You can experiment like this with any shot you want to master. Remember to stay down and follow through every shot. You will improve much faster like this.

Practice like a scientist; detached from the results yet very observant so you can make the proper adjustments. With concentrated effort you will see great improvement.

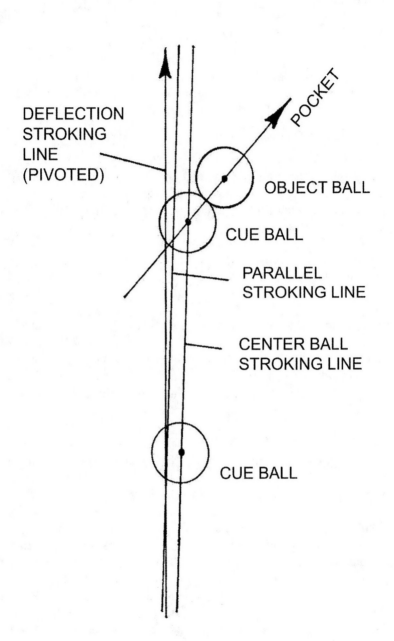

DEFLECTION
STROKING
LINE
(PIVOTED)

POCKET

OBJECT BALL

CUE BALL

PARALLEL
STROKING LINE

CENTER BALL
STROKING LINE

CUE BALL

LONG AND STRAIGHT

All world class players have a stroke on which they can rely most of the time. When they concentrate on a target and set up their stance, they are confident in delivering the cue ball on the path it needs to travel for success.

I like to compare the stroke and stance (including the bridge hand) to a large machine gun on a tripod. The machine gun will not be too effective if the tripod is wobbly or off balance, and the tripod will not help much if the machine gun is not too powerful or does not shoot too straight.

As you develop your stance into a solid entity that stays solid, even during the delivery of your final stroke, you will now have the opportunity to create a really straight and dependable stroke.

Perhaps the best way to create a straight stroke is to repeatedly shoot "long straight in" shots (see diagram on page 72). Using a rail bridge, I like to set the cue ball about 8-15 inches off the end rail and put the object ball about one diamond on the other side of the side pocket. Make sure they are lined perfectly straight into the far pocket when lining them up.

To get any lasting benefit from the drill, you should do it for fifteen minutes minimum every day for two weeks. Once you get good at it, just a rack or two of fifteen balls a day to keep sharp is good…whatever it takes. When doing this drill, you really want to isolate your stroke as much as possible. This means to separate your stroke from your body. You will need to pay attention to your body as you do this, feeling for any unnecessary movements during your stroke. If you tend to move your body (head included), the pain of missing should train you to keep still.

You really need to try and give freedom to your stroking arm. With each ball you shoot, your stance should become more and more still. Eventually, you need to feel this on your own without the watchful eye of someone else.

Ideally, you want to pocket the ball clean, and stop the cue ball instantly with zero side spin. Stroking this shot really hard will help you develop a great stroke. Any slight errors you commit will be compounded when hitting hard. The cue ball will deflect more with accidental sidespin and the pocket will be more likely to jaw the object ball. This will put a premium on your precise delivery.

Focus on a nice, slow, smooth backswing, pulling straight back from the object ball, and then throw (without letting go) the cue stick right towards the object ball. You can also look at the center of the cue ball during your stroke, as that will produce good results too if you are lined up well.

Try to have the attitude of detachment from the outcome of the shot and just focus on your stroke. This will help your body stay still and increase your self awareness. Just let your stroke out, for better or worse, and make any adjustments you might want on the next shot.

Once you start smacking the object ball to the back of the pocket and stopping the cue ball with regularity, just keep doing it over and over, really engraining it into your being. You can then ease up on the speed and try "draw and follow" as well.

Your improvement in those categories will be proportional to the work you put into this drill as well. One beautiful thing about this drill is that it helps tremendously with all areas of your game. The "long straight in" can be one of your game's best friends.

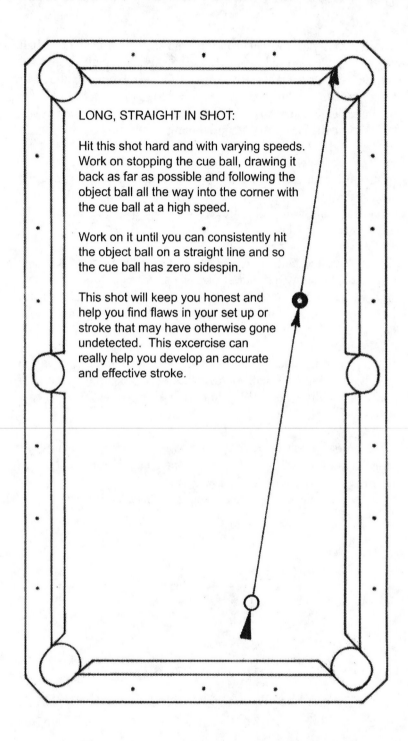

LONG, STRAIGHT IN SHOT:

Hit this shot hard and with varying speeds.
Work on stopping the cue ball, drawing it
back as far as possible and following the
object ball all the way into the corner with
the cue ball at a high speed.

Work on it until you can consistently hit
the object ball on a straight line and so
the cue ball has zero sidespin.

This shot will keep you honest and
help you find flaws in your set up or
stroke that may have otherwise gone
undetected. This excercise can
really help you develop an accurate
and effective stroke.

AUTOMATIC STROKE POWER ADDITION

There are many beginners to intermediate players out there who learn to play good pool to a certain level, yet when they really need a little power in their game, they just cannot deliver what is required for the shot. This problem could cause shots that only require a medium or medium-hard shot to be out of reach.

In this article I will cover one quick fix that may just be the boost they are looking for. It will seem so basic; yet without detection by a keen eye, players may never detect this during their entire pool playing life. Let's see if this could be you, and if it is, let me know if you break through an old ceiling on your power game.

When you throw a baseball for distance, how do you begin? You wind up, right? You pull your hand and arm to as far back a position as you can, and then you begin your accelerating throwing motion that eventually launches the ball. In pool, you begin your stroke with the backswing.

And so the problem I'm talking about here is that many players fail to pull back their cue as far as possible on their backswing when they need power! They will ask me why they cannot draw the ball very far or get much action on the cue ball and when I watch them, I see that they are only pulling their cue back halfway before beginning their final stroke forward! This is like trying to throw a baseball for distance, but starting by only holding the ball up by your forehead, and then trying to launch it 50 yards.

If this applies to you, try pulling your cue all the way back so that the ferrule is in the closed part of your bridge or on top of your thumb with an open hand bridge. When you pull back all the way like this, it gives you the ability to have more power with less effort. It gives you the ability to accelerate smoothly, and more time to accelerate so your timing into the cue ball is just right. It will allow you to hit the ball without jabbing at it with a sudden punchy motion. Your stroke will look a lot smoother, and it will be easier for you to get a nice long follow through which is also extremely important.

At the back of your backswing, be careful not to drop your grip hand too low. This will cause your tip to have a real downward arcing motion into the cue ball without much follow through, and may cause many miscues on draw shots unless your timing is impeccable. It is much easier to have your hand up a little higher on the end of your back swing so the tip is low on its way into the cue ball, and the cue is also on a good plane for a nice long follow through.

Be sure not to negate your nice back swing by stopping your stroke at the cue ball. Allow the tip to follow through several inches beyond the cue ball. Keeping your grip hand somewhat loose will help you to follow through with ease. Let this entire motion, from backswing to follow through, be one long and smooth motion. Test to see how you can vary the speed by changing your back swing and get more power by pulling back as far as possible.

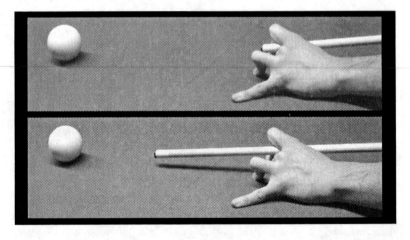

In the top photo you can get more cue ball power with less forward "effort," and your motion will be more of a "stroke" than a "shove." (Photo courtesy of Jeremy Wheat)

Pulling back all the way will give you room to accelerate through the cue ball.

A half backswing like this will limit your power, but is ok on softer shots as long as you still deliver a smooth stroke and follow-through. (Photos: Jeremy Wheat)

Ideally, the stroking forearm is vertical when the cue tip strikes cue ball.

SOFTLY NOW

How can you hit the cue ball very softly and still get a good stroke and follow-through? Well, the idea behind a regular stroke is to be accelerating through the cue ball, like you are throwing the cue ball through it. If you need to hit the cue ball very softly and you take a full backswing, you will have to decelerate or have a slow monotonous stroke in order to get a soft hit. This could take away from your touch.

To get a nice soft hit, take a short or very short backswing. One way to accomplish this is by moving your bridge hand to within just inches of the cue ball. Or you could have your normal length bridge but just do not pull your cue back all the way to your bridge hand (see middle photo on page 75).

Notice that when you are just trying to touch the cue ball and not really move it, you put your cue tip right next to the cue ball before striking it. How far you pull your backswing back for different soft speeds depends mainly on the feel you develop as you play more and more.

In order to develop your soft shot backswing distances and touch, here are a couple of useful drills. The first one I call "teeter-totter." The idea is to hit the object ball so softly that it travels to the lip of the pocket and hesitates before dropping. You want to pocket the ball at the softest speed possible. Practice shots of all distances between both the object ball and the pocket, and the cue ball and object ball. Also set up shots of all different angles. If you are not familiar with this, I suspect you will be surprised at just how softly you can hit the ball and still make it.

The other drill is to shoot towards random object balls with the goal of having the cue ball barely make it to that ball, touch it, and remain frozen to it or stay within four inches or less distance from it after contact. Practice this from all distances and even with kick shots of one or more rails (a kick is where the cue ball strikes a rail before hitting the object ball). These drills will certainly make you a better-rounded player.

Professional Pool Player Akiko Kitayama "Leopard Woman" of Japan demonstrates solid massé shot fundamentals. Akiko is an excellent player who brings style and flair to the sport. (Photo courtesy of Akiko Kitayama)

BUILD SKILL AND CONFIDENCE

First of all, congratulations to John Schmidt for recently running 400 balls in Straight Pool on a 9-foot table! Not 399, not 401, but 400 balls! Wow! John modestly told me he may never break that number, but I think he could beat Mosconi's world record run of 526 balls. Who knows, could he run 1,000? Could you run 1,000?

After his 400 ball run, Schmidt posted a run of 245 and captured it on video (it recently came out for sale). I know John to be a total class act and definitely skilled enough to accomplish such feats. I've heard stories about how he used to wake up every morning while in Seattle and eat 100 ball runs for breakfast! John is an all around great, as he is a 9-ball and One Pocket Champion as well.

Straight pool is a game that requires tremendous cue ball control, shot-making ability, knowledge, strategizing, concentration, rhythm, and a positive attitude. You will be doing yourself a service by learning and trying to improve in this game.

I am now going to give you a game or drill I created for myself when I was a kid that really helped me advance quickly in pool. It is good for players of all skill levels for different reasons. Here it is:

Evenly spread all 15 balls across the table, with a few balls close to the rail but not too many. Then, with cue ball in hand on the first shot, run the balls in any order you choose. When you run out without scratching, set the balls back on the table in a similar fashion and do it again. Keep going until you miss. That constitutes one game or run for you.

The object is to pick a target number you wish to run, and go for it. This is considerably easier than regulation straight pool, but it can present a great challenge and opportunity to build skill and confidence.

For a beginning player, running just one table can be a great accomplishment and milestone. It will require an understanding of aim and the ability to hit the contact point. Some basic cue ball skill will help, but it is possible to run the table once with excellent pocketing and some lucky positional play with no scratching.

Running two tables with no cue ball control is unlikely. It is just difficult to keep getting lucky. So to run multiple tables, you will need pocketing skills and cue ball skills. It also takes analytical skills for evaluating which shots to shoot.

The more racks you want to run, the more skill you will need. Once clearing the table becomes easy for you, posting high numbers will mainly be a matter of concentration and execution.

I figured early on that running 100 balls should be routine. But I was learning still and I had to work hard at getting there. The more I played this game the easier it got, and so did running 200 and more. It was after this that I switched to playing regular straight pool, but coming back to this drill can be helpful and fun.

The key is to give yourself a target number that sounds like a challenge to you. Once you get that number, you set the bar higher. I forget my record at this game, but how many can you run?

A lot of times you may find your run ended on an easy miss or loss of concentration. Well, that should aggravate you enough to concentrate better on your next try. All the while you will be learning and recognizing patterns on the table, and you will be eliminating the errors that caused previous blunders. Your skill will be improving.

This also gives you practice in dealing with the self-imposed pressure to reach a target number. Even though the tables are just as easy as in the beginning, you may feel more pressure as you get close to your target number and beyond. Dealing with this will make you tougher under the pressure of competition.

This helps your confidence because once you start regularly clearing the table; your mindset in other games like 8-Ball, 9-Ball and Straight-Pool will be to *run the table*! Once you play this game a bit, you will realize just how amazing it is to run 400 balls in regulation straight pool. Way to go John! Keep running!

Here is John Schmidt "Mr. 400" en route to winning the 2006 US Open 9-Ball Championships in Chesapeake, VA. (Photo Courtesy of www.jrcalvert.com)

WOW CHIA-CHING

Chia-Ching Wu of Taiwan. To watch him play 9-Ball, you really would not be surprised to see him win the World 9-Ball Championship. He's got good form, a straight stroke, steady rhythm, great shot-making, excellent cue ball control, smart patterns, poise, an awesome break, and a ton of confidence.

Oh yeah, and he's sixteen years old. Sixteen years old? Are you kidding me? Actually, skilled and talented teenaged pool players are not extremely uncommon, but good enough to win the world title? And then if such a kid is good enough…to actually get out there and do it? That's incredible! More than well done kid; you just rewrote the pool history books!

Johnny Archer was the previous youngest world champion at 21, surprise- surprise. And I was impressed to see Thorsten Hohmann win it in 2003 at 24 years of age. But 16 years old, really? You are not kidding me?

Most people are asking me if this kid really plays that good. I'd say yes. I had the thrill of watching him win the tournament in person. It is amazing enough that a 16-year-old won, but how he did it was more incredible and has undoubtedly won him countless lifetime fans.

In the race-to-17 finals, losing 16-12, he had ball in hand on the 2 ball after the 27-year-old Kuo's untimely no-rail foul, and ran that rack to make the score 16-13. Needing to win 4 games in a row, the 16-year-old Wu proceeded to break and run precisely 4 racks of 9-ball on pool's greatest stage, in the most urgent of all moments.

To top it off, Wu made the final, hill-hill championship winning 9-ball with a mechanical bridge! It was not an easy shot (at least for me) into a small pocket, but he just asked for the bridge, lined it up and shot it in—piece of cake. He raised both his cue and the bridge into the air, screamed with everyone else, smiled ear to ear (he could not wipe it off), and the value of his bobble-head dolls just went way up.

I was up in the press box next to fellow pro players Rico Diks and Corey Deuel during the finals. I think we were more nervous than Wu was. Corey said to me after Wu won, "That was the most amazing thing in pool I've ever seen."

This tops my list too, barely edging out Earl Strickland's brilliant 1-9 combo to run his 10th consecutive rack and $1,000,000 in the 1996 Dallas Million Dollar Challenge.

Wu plays just the kind of 9-ball that is fun to play and fun to watch. Attack, attack, attack… He goes for just about everything, and expects to make everything. After watching him for a while, you expect him to make everything, too.

Top Australian pro David Reljik was telling me, "If he has a weakness, it is his safety play, but even that's not bad. His attack game is just incredible." Starting out playing snooker as a kid must have helped his skill and confidence in shot-making. He plays good position, too, with a soft touch and plenty of power when he needs it.

The thing that impresses me most about Chia-Ching is his confidence. At any age, to play with his confidence is awesome. Even if Efren Reyes did what he did, people would be talking about it forever.

I hope a lot of kids see Wu's victory here in the States. Video game sales may take a hit, with pool cue sales making a big jump. The score: Pool-1, Video Games-0. Come on kids, unplug your mind from your television set and start playing pool! Congratulations, Chia-Ching Wu! You're the man!

Chia-Ching Wu won both the 2005 World 9-Ball Championship and the 2005 World 8-Ball Championship. Amazingly, he won both of these titles when he was only sixteen years old! He will be around for a while. (Photo courtesy of Raul Roa & rpsports.com)

WU PROVES WORTHY

There just are not enough sports writers in pool, so I have to cover the continuing exploits of Taiwan's wonder boy, Chia-Ching Wu. Can you imagine anyone (Efren Reyes and Nick Varner don't count) winning two world titles in less than five months? Well, Wu has done it again! In November, 2005, sixteen-year-old phenomenon Chia-Ching Wu won the WPA World 8-Ball Title in Fujairah in the U.A.E.(United Arab Emirates), adding to his already unimaginable victory in July, 2005, at the World 9-Ball Championships.

I've heard a report that the Taiwanese government gave him a $200,000 bonus for this latest victory to add to the $20,000 first prize. He also doubled his bonus from Knight Shot, one of his sponsors based in the UAE, who supplied the tables for the World 8-Ball Championships.

It is great to have a government that values their world champion pool players and rewards them for a job well done. You have to admit, the kid deserves it. He just achieved one of the toughest things in the sports world. Because I had an early exit from the event, all I could do was watch and I was impressed with his 8-Ball game.

I have heard from one source that he had never played 8-Ball before and learned the patterns by watching other players play their matches. Hmm, that sounds like a stretch but who knows? His nickname is the "Boy Genius" after all.

It was somewhat of a miracle event for him as he had a few hill-hill matches with the most notable escape coming in the quarter finals when Thorsten Hohmann surprisingly missed an easy 8-Ball at hill-hill. From there, Wu took his good omen and then dominated Niels Feijen 10-5 in the semis and Nick Van Den Berg 11-3 in the finals.

Earlier in the tournament, I was watching Alex Lely playing some great 8-Ball on Wu with a 7-3 lead when he somehow gave Wu a shot. Wu proceeded to run rack after rack with smart patterns and brilliant shot-making as he breezed past Lely to win the match. It seems like the score does not matter to Wu, as he will just cruise forward in high gear with calmness, focus and confidence.

A celebrity in Taiwan, he is known for being a nice kid and humble. With his newfound wealth, he has bought his grandmother a house to say thanks for all the hard work in bringing him up.

Wu is the undisputed Champion of the World for 2005 with his two WPA world titles. Chia-Ching Wu joins an elite group of players who have won both the World 8-Ball and 9-Ball Titles including Nick Varner, Efren Reyes and Earl Strickland, and Ronnie Alcano who just won both World Titles in the 2006-2007 season.

Without a doubt, Wu's two WPA World Titles in 2005 are incredible and meaningful, especially with such a deep field of top international talent. Great playing, Wu. Keep on playing!

Nick Varner, an 8-time World Champion and mental master, locks in on his target in a classic photo from earlier in his career. Varner is the only player ever to have won World Titles in five games (Straight Pool, 8-Ball, 9-Ball, Bank Pool, and One-Pocket) and is a legitimate candidate for "Greatest Pool Player of All Time." Nick has come up with some of my favorite quotes: "I used to go to a tournament and just look at what first place paid to see how much money I was going to make that week." "The more I practice, the luckier I get." "I like that stage towards the end of a tournament where I'm so in stroke that the pockets look like buckets." "I just always like to try one hundred percent." (Photo courtesy of www.nickvarner.com)

YOUR BACKSWING SETS UP
YOUR STROKE

So many times, I have written about the importance of knowing the stroking line and setting up your stance based on knowing and seeing this line. Anyone who is playing well has a keen awareness of the stroking line and has a nice balance on this line. So my question now is "How do you keep your cue on this line?"

A common malady among players who approach me for advice is that their cue wobbles side-to-side while they are taking their practice strokes. Of course, the first fix to this is to know the stroking line before your bend into your stance so that your eyes and hands (and cue) are on the line at the moment you arrive in your stance. If you do not take care of this part first, you will miss much more often.

So, once you have tried in earnest from the get go to get your eyes and cue on the stroking line *before* and as you complete your form, you now need a way to keep them there in your warm-up strokes and during your all important actual stroke. This takes work, trust, talent, and/or years of practice. That's ok; that is what keeps a pool player's blood pumping. All of that is as natural to improving as breathing is to living. It is best if you enjoy every breath and every step on your road to pool mastery as well.

I like to draw comparisons between pool and archery. One of the top books I recommend to my pool students is *Zen in the Art of Archery* by Eugen Herrigel.

I have also had the fortune to talk with a champion archer in California while at a party a couple years ago. He explained to me how he sets up his shots, and I was amazed at how similar the process was to a champion cueist's setup. First, he set his feet. Next he drew the bow with it pointed to the ground slightly. Then, with the bow already drawn and his head in place, he lifted up by bending his waist with his eyes on the target and pointed his arrow at the target. Wow! So similar to effective pool technique!

Pool is more than hand-eye coordination; it is *hands*-eye coordination (and actually body-eye coordination). Both of your hands need to coordinate to what you are looking at. Hopefully you do an excellent job of placing and keeping your bridge hand where it needs to be. Your grip hand is slightly more complicated, to say the least, as it will be in almost constant motion.

Try to keep that motion on the stroking line; not just on your forward stroke, but also on your back swing. Just imagine how much easier it will be to begin moving your cue forward on a line if you begin that motion precisely on the line you want it to travel down.

Instead of having your stroke find the straight line after it begins moving, why not have it start moving forward from a point that is already on the line? So, I want you to try concentrating extra hard on pulling your backswing back perfectly on the stroking line and see how this affects the ease with which you are able to stroke forward on a straight line. Even experiment with pausing at the end of your back swing, making sure that the back of your cue is on the stroking line.

As you pull your cue back, have your eyes forward either on the "ghost" cue ball, the "ghost" spot on the table, the contact point on the object ball, or on the stroking line. As long as you concentrate with extra effort on keeping your backswing on the stroking line, stroking forward with accuracy will seem to come with more ease.

Eventually, this will become second nature and the wobble in your stroke, if there is any, should diminish or disappear depending on the work and body awareness you apply to what you are doing. Make it a relaxed yet focused effort and have confidence that you will improve.

By keeping your eyes on the target during your backswing, you will begin your forward stroke with your cue in an ideal place; on the stroking line. Notice that your author's eyes are looking ahead toward the object ball. If you have a nicely-grooved stroke, you can easily make your shot if you close your eyes at the end of the backswing. If you did not look at the object ball while pulling back, it would be trickier to make the ball with your eyes closed. Test this for yourself. (Photo courtesy of Jeremy Wheat)

THROW YOUR CUE

What is your definition of a stroke? In the words of the distinguished and world renowned instructor Jerry Briesath, a stroke is "a beautiful throwing motion, with the cue tip ending four to six inches past the cue ball," or words to that effect. Doesn't that paint a clearer picture in your head of a stroke? While your follow-through does not have to fit perfectly into the four to six inch distance, the image in your mind should be helpful.

Many people have the inclination to jab or poke the cue ball by stopping or pulling back the cue stick shortly after striking the cue ball. How effective would a baseball pitcher be if she yanked back her hand shortly after releasing the ball? A throw requires acceleration, and a follow-through is a natural byproduct of this requirement. I believe a follow-through will also allow the cue tip to make contact with the cue ball slightly longer and give it more spin when needed, as will a slower speed of stroke.

By throwing your cue stick through the cue ball, you will naturally follow through. Your stroking arm will also be more relaxed with a smooth throwing motion, giving you a better chance for success. Of course do not actually let go of the cue when you throw it, just allow your hand to keep moving forward like a child on a swing-set who swings forward and up without letting go. Like the child on the swing set, your hand will also swing up, causing the cue tip to go down into the table. This is OK.

To make your stroke longer, drop your elbow slightly as your hand swings upward. Dropping your elbow *after* your hand starts swinging upward is especially good for follow shots or just to lengthen your stroke. You can also keep pushing your grip hand forward without swinging it up (see photo on page 42). Rule of thumb: Experiment and closely watch the stroking arm of many different great players. If the cue ball is close to the object ball, or if it is going to spin back quickly into the path of your cue tip, then you may have to jerk back or stop your stroke short out of necessity. For the most part, allow yourself to throw your cue stick through the cue ball with a complete and smooth follow-through.

READY, AIM, FIRE!

You will not be ready to bend down on a shot until you have decided exactly what you are trying to execute. First you want to know your strategy in relation to the lay of the table, and then you want to know your strategy in relation to this shot that faces you now.

In his book *Smart Pool! The Mind Game*, John Delaveau thoroughly and convincingly outlines the importance of pre-shot planning and thinking, before concentrating on the shot itself. I highly recommend this book to anyone interested in getting better and being more consistent.

So now that you are ready, you must aim. Aiming includes the entire formation of the stance, all the way through your final stroke, where you are fixed on the stroking line and ready to fire. It is pointless to get ready, aim, and then jump up as you stroke the cue.

Yet so many players do this, revealing their lack of confidence in their preparation, readiness and aiming. Once you tie the knot of holy matrimony between your plan and stance (aim), you must be faithful in your delivery of the cue. If it does not feel right, stand up and re-marry. Soon enough, your preparations will be as easy as getting married in Las Vegas and you will be able to move mountains if you just have faith enough to stay in your stance as you stroke your cue. Ready, Aim, Fire!

BREAKING THE BODY MOVEMENT BARRIER

Across pool tables everywhere, people carefully line up on their shots slowly and deliberately, measuring up through a series of practice strokes, only to lurch forward and upward at the precise moment when the cue ball is struck, as if jarred by a massive bolt of electricity.

Players who jump up—and there are many who do (to varying degrees)—are often baffled and discouraged by their lack of consistency. Perhaps this tendency is motivated by a subconscious intention to "help" the ball into the pocket, but in reality it is the perpetrator of such bad form that requires help.

Quite simply, with the exception of the break shot, one's body should be completely still throughout the warm-up and delivery of a shot while allowing the shooting arm to perform all the work.

Even at the professional level, a high percentage of missed shots are accompanied by sudden body movement (SBM) at the point of delivery. SBM may be nothing more than theatrical response to the "surprise of missing"—a reflex that captures the hope of making a shot and the reality of missing it. But in most cases, SBM is as much the cause of a misguided cue ball as it is the effect. Let us then examine the reason for SBM and what can be done to minimize its damaging consequences.

Be prepared. SBM is often the manifestation of an attempt to correct one's aim at the last second. This can be avoided through a disciplined effort to refrain from "pulling the trigger" until comfort and certainty are achieved.

Take it easy. Optimum performance in pool can only be achieved when relaxed. Tense muscles operate adversely to a smooth stroke. This is particularly true when a muscle spasm triggers a SBM at the moment of delivery. Alternately expanding and contracting your muscles is an effective relaxation technique.

Breathing exercises, stretching, and regular visits to a masseuse are also beneficial. For the true devotee, transcendental meditation is an excellent vehicle for mental and spiritual relaxation.

Keep the faith. Anxiety, doubt and fear can cause one to jump up on key shots in high pressure situations. The higher the stakes, the harder it is to regulate these feelings. Once again, breathe deeply, attempt to divorce yourself from the outcome of a shot, lose your self image while playing (become the shot), have faith, pray, smile, and channel any hindering emotions into positive body language and concentration.

Take your time. Have you ever missed a ball because you were on your way to the next shot in mid stroke? Whoa Nelly! Settle down and see each shot through to its conclusion. Form good habits. While a handful of excellent players exhibit slight SBM regularly, it is usually only a small movement that does not interfere with their stroke too much. Many more players fail to realize their potential because of this tendency and not keeping in control.

Of course I recommend not moving at all. Save the theatrics for mime class and build the good habit of staying down on every shot and only moving your arm. One helpful practice exercise involves staying down and frozen until the cue ball comes to a complete stop.

In game situations, make a habit of staying down until the object ball falls into the pocket. Ask your sparring partner to alert you to SBM, as habits are partially unconscious by definition.

The discipline of keeping your body still on every shot will improve your shot-making, accuracy, cue ball control, length of inning, and ultimately the enjoyment you derive from the game.

Here is your author staying still on a shot. Notice that the right arm, cue, and cue ball are the only moving objects. Keep your body still! (Photo courtesy of Charles Pinkett)

Here your author is still down with a completed follow-through when the cue ball makes contact with the object ball. To discipline yourself to stay down, do not move until the cue ball comes to a complete stop on every shot for a few racks. Exaggerating your "stay down" period in practice could help turn you into a more solid player overall. (Photo by author)

ARE YOU READY?

Mike Sigel once said he never shot until he was ready, and back in his heyday, he did very little missing. Once at the U.S. Open 9-Ball, he told me and Charlie Williams, "Back then I didn't miss." All he had to do was show up at a tournament in order to win. Possibly a slight exaggeration from Mike "The Mouth," but based on his record, not too far from the truth.

Have you ever stroked a shot even though you knew or felt you were not aiming correctly? Only to exclaim "I knew I was going to miss that!" in an attempt to justify your result? It may be true that every pool player who has ever missed has experienced this feeling at one time or another.

Conversely, it may also be true that every pool player who has ever made a ball has had the feeling of knowing that a particular ball was going into the pocket.

If you are going about the business of pocketing balls and running out, it would be to your advantage to eliminate the feelings that you will miss a shot. Doing this requires a respectable amount of patience and discipline, especially in regards to those moments of uncertainty.

In the past, I have dealt with this situation by shooting anyway because I just couldn't wait. I was in a hurry to make the ball and run the table. Upon missing such a shot, I would feel thoroughly betrayed and disgusted.

One can only take so much pain before the change response takes effect, and with experience and maturity I have learned to stand up and start over in those rare occasions when my aim does not feel correct. This takes a good deal of patience.

While it takes patience to stand up if the shot does not feel right, it takes discipline to minimize those uncertain moments. Discipline in terms of a pre-shot routine including: clarity of your intended outcome, positive body language, finding the aiming point, body positioning, warm-up strokes and eye movement routine, and keeping your body still upon delivery of your actual stroke.

By having a pre-shot routine or SOP (Standard Operating Procedure), your feelings of knowing a ball will drop will increase, and you will be more equipped to create rhythm and run out consistently.

If after all this you still aren't ready, either stand up or take some extra strokes without over doing it, until your shot is "on." Figure out a formula that works for you. How good would you be if you only shot when you were ready?

Thorsten Hohmann "The Hitman" of Germany has a run in Straight Pool of 404 balls. After Basic Training in the German Army, Thorsten's service was to play pool in the Special Sports program where he immersed in the game for 4 years and mastered his technique. He emerged in 2003 to win the World Pool Championship at 24 years of age and has since won the 2006 World 14.1 Championship, and the 2006 IPT North American Open Championship, landing him a cool $350,000. (Photo courtesy of Mark Whiteside)

THE LANDING STRIP

If you were about to walk a tight wire across a thousand-foot deep ravine, would you step onto the wire from the side or from straight on? Personally, I would want to be looking straight down the wire before stepping onto it. I would not step onto the wire from the side, and then while I am wobbling onto it, try to find the line and my balance. Or let's say you are a pilot trying to land a jumbo jet. Would you touch down on the runway at a slight angle and then try to turn the plane straight once the wheels were down? I didn't think so. You would approach the runway perfectly straight while in the air and just try to hold that straight line on the landing.

In pool, the stroking line is your tight wire or landing strip (see diagram on page 99). Pretend you are a pilot and that you must find this line while you are standing, just before you get into your stance.

Now, once your eyes are on the line, keep them there, all the way into your stance. You are coming in for a landing on the stroking line and once you are down, your stance will be correctly balanced for a smooth delivery.

Or, while you are standing, pretend you are about to walk the tight rope and that you want to be looking directly down the wire before and as you take your first step. A solid pool stance is built around the stroking line, so it is necessary to first see this line and keep it in your sights while you line up.

The purpose of imagining a "ghost cue ball" is to help you find the stroking line. The ghost cue ball is located where the real cue ball will be at the moment of contact with the object ball you are trying to pocket.

With a center ball hit (anywhere on the cue ball's vertical axis), the stroking line runs right down the center of the real cue ball and the ghost cue ball. Whatever trick you can conceive of to accurately find this line will work. My preference is to find the spot on the table where the ghost ball is resting and use that as the end of my "landing strip." The spot I use is about the size of a small pea. This spot is also on the line of centers (it basically is the center of the ghost cue ball, just dropped down to the table) between the ghost cue ball and the object ball that leads to a specific part of the pocket.

So my first step is actually to find what spot in the pocket I want the object ball to enter, and then extend a line from there through the center of the object ball and out the other side. Now I know my spot will intersect this line, and all I have to do is make sure it is one ball's radius (1⅛ inches) from the edge of the object ball.

Once I have this spot, I know where the runway is and that it is time to come in for a landing into my stance. Once I am locked into my stance, I stop looking at the spot on the table and only look at the actual contact point on the object ball.

Now, even though the contact point is not on the stroking line, my stroke is in place, and with muscle memory and feel, I can send the cue ball down the tight wire to the target.

Although very strange at first, it is also possible to look at the cue ball last and in essence this is looking down the stroking line. Enjoy the process of finding what works best for you.

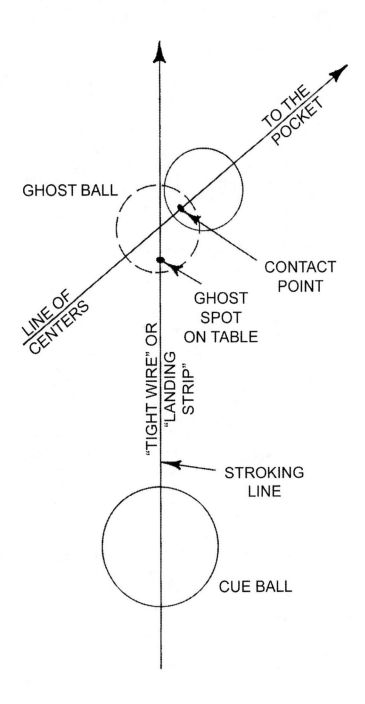

TO THE POCKET

GHOST BALL

LINE OF CENTERS

CONTACT POINT

GHOST SPOT ON TABLE

"TIGHT WIRE" OR "LANDING STRIP"

STROKING LINE

CUE BALL

SLICE AND DICE

The ability to make thin "cut shots" down the rail will win you many games and matches. "Cut shots" or "thin slices" are when the cue ball needs to just graze the edge of the object ball to send it towards the pocket. You have got to be able to pocket the ball and also, just as important, control the cue ball. You never want to just go for the cut and not plan your cue ball destination. That would go against one of the first things my grandfather taught me, "Never turn the cue ball loose." The good news is that with an exact center ball hit, or just slightly above center, you can contain the cue ball quite nicely in between the rails (see the diagram on page 102). Hitting the cue ball below center may cause a scratch in one of the side pockets, unless the cut is close to 90 degrees from the line of centers.

First, we will discuss making the cut. For one, the margin for error is small because small changes in the line of aim cause more deviation from the contact point when compared to a straighter shot. Keeping that in mind will help you concentrate and be disciplined in your approach.

The ability to stroke straight and hit center ball will really help you slice (cut) a ball thin. The first key, as in all shot-making, is to set up carefully on the stroking line. On a thin cut, the stroking line will not pass through the object ball and if you are not familiar with this shot, it will almost seem like you are aiming to miss the ball.

If you are cutting the ball to the right, look on the cloth to the left of the object ball and find the spot on the table where you think the cue ball will be resting at the moment it contacts the object ball (Spot A in the diagram on page 102). This is your aiming point. Now keep your eyes on that spot as you set up your cue and your stance on the line between that spot and center ball.

Once you get in your stance, double check during your practice strokes to see that you are actually aiming on that line. Once you are confident with the line, you can go ahead and deliver the stroke *on that line.*

I like to look at the contact point at the edge of the ball when I pull the trigger, but because this point is not on or near the stroking line, I still focus my feel on stroking straight on the stroking line. It is important to trust your stroke and deliver it as relaxed and smooth as possible.

You could experiment with just looking at the spot when you stroke. That will get you used to stroking towards a point clear off the edge of the ball. If the object ball is near the rail, I like to extend the tangent line of the cue ball beyond the table to some target in the room even with the cloth (Spot B). I know that if I can carom the cue ball straight towards that target, the object ball will go in the pocket.

It is a handy skill to make the cue ball travel straight across the table back and forth once it slices in the object ball. This becomes easier once you hit the object ball parallel to the rail because that will make your tangent line perpendicular to the rail, giving you a natural back and forth direction. Often, somewhere along that line will give you good position for the next shot.

It is just a matter of controlling the speed after first picking (1) exactly how many times you want to cross the table and (2) the exact spot on which to stop for position. I actually count how many times I want it to cross the table, and pick the exact spot (Spot C). You have to go through in your mind the path of the cue ball, and how fast it is moving initially, and how long it will take to decelerate.

I gave the cue ball line a slight angle in the diagram so you can see how many times it crosses the table. Once you get confident with making the cut, controlling the speed also gets easier.

Cut shots are a nice alternative to banks because if you just hit the ball in the right direction, it will usually go in the pocket regardless of how hard you hit the cue ball. Bank shots are much more sensitive to speed and spin from the cue ball.

Working on really thin cuts in practice will give you a whole new set of options to choose from during your matches. Remember to relax and be smooth down the stroking line at all cue ball speeds.

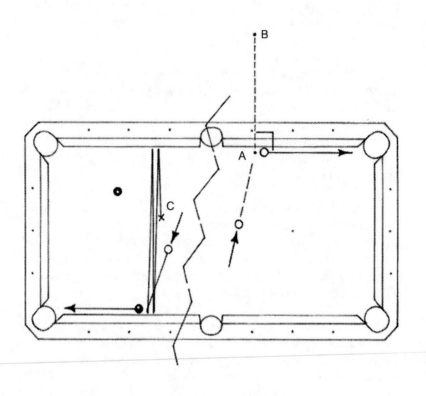

See how the stroking line is set up completely off of the object ball on a thin cut? Stroke down this line and let the edge of the cue ball contact the edge of the object ball. The only time your stroking line will actually intersect the object ball on a thin cut shot like this is when you are using inside english (left english from the author's view in the photo), in which case the cue ball will be deflected away from the stroking line and still strike the object ball on the contact point. Master making these cuts without side spin, and then start experimenting with side spin. (Photos courtesy of Jeremy Wheat)

POWER BREAK

Forget the soft break for now; instead, I have a couple tips for you to help you break with more accuracy and power. Since you will be hitting the balls hard, your stance needs to be more stable than ever.

So often overlooked is the bridge hand, which is a third of the tripod formed also by your feet. Breaking from the rail is good not only because the angle of approach on the one ball (the head ball of the rack in 9-Ball) is conducive to pocketing balls, you can also get really solid with your hand on the rail.

I do this by planting the heel of my hand (palm) onto the table as well as my fingers. This really allows me to put my weight into my arm and table which makes my tripod really solid; and solid is good, good, good.

One key is to keep the weight into your palm even on your backswing. You don't want to sway backwards with your backswing and ease up on the pressure into the table with your bridge hand. So, especially with your last backswing, lean forward into your bridge hand as you pull the cue back.

When you start your swing into and through the cue ball, your hand will already be snugly in place, allowing you to exert your sledgehammer break into the stack.

After you contact the cue ball it is OK to take your hand off the table in classic Johnny Archer style, but not before. Or just leave your hand there and follow through like Earl Strickland.

When breaking from the bed of the table, you also want your bridge palm planted snugly into the table with some more of your body weight than usual. You can even turn your hand more sideways and clump your fingers together to make a more solid bridge.

Another thing I like to do is look at the cue ball during my actual break stroke. Because, really, you need to hit the cue ball really hard; not the rack. So I concentrate on lining up accurately and getting balanced in my set up and warm up strokes, and once I think I'm on line and solid enough, I'll look at the cue ball and send it. Yet you can also have success looking at the head ball.

I also like to bring my front foot closer to the stroking line when I break. This allows me to shift my weight forward and keep my balance at the same time. Also, push forward with your back leg and foot and drive your cue forward as you stroke through the cue ball. See if any of these recommendations add power and accuracy to your break.

Your author breaks a 9-Ball rack from the bed of the table at the Bicycle Club & Casino in Los Angeles at the 2004 UPA Tour Championships. Notice how the left hand is still planted into the table as the body is pushed forward with the back foot. Try to keep your bridge hand very solid at least until you strike the cue ball. (Photo courtesy of Paul Hyman)

Before you pull back to swing your break stroke, try putting some weight into your bridge hand. You can test the solidity of your bridge hand by supporting your weight on it as your author illustrates below. You could perform the same test for your non-break bridges as well. Have fun with this one! (Photos courtesy of Jeremy Wheat)

KEEPING A LEAD

As important as I know it is to bear down until the end of the match, even when I have a big lead, sometimes it takes a painful loss to remind me that it is not over till it's over, baby. At the UPA Tour stop in Pittsburgh, PA., I had a comfortable 8-2 lead in a race to 11 over Mike Davis on the one loss side with the winner advancing to the final eight players.

Mike was not playing his game and I seemed to be coasting along to a win. Mike, being the great player he is, kept coming at me and made some really good jump shots along the way. But even if he started playing perfectly the odds were against him, as it was alternate break and I would be guaranteed at least a few more chances.

I started watching the other 3 matches in that round, and seemed to drop my guard a bit on one key shot on the 3 ball that I had to elevate my cue for, and missed. I should have taken a bit more time and given a better effort.

Then, on my first chance to win the set on the hill, I was down on a shot when a strand of hair fell in my eye bothering me and I stayed down anyway and missed the ball. Mike ran out. I should have stood up and moved the hair out of my eyes, and now I was mad at myself for being so attached to shooting at that moment.

I had another chance on the hill and miscued on a long draw shot, making the ball but ending up short on position. Mike won that game. At hill-hill, Mike barely missed a tough shot on the one ball, but slopped the 7 in and ran out, winning the set.

He did what he needed to do; forgot the past and played hard, and I lost just enough focus to allow him the needed opportunities to win the set.

Usually, if I have a huge lead, I play even harder because I know just how possible comebacks are, especially for a great player. Also, as many times as I have come from behind to win, I am usually on guard against that happening to me. It might help to pretend that you are losing when you do have that big lead.

It had been a long time since I had blown a big lead, and now that this happened I will not forget the lesson for a long time—and hopefully never! Congratulations to Mike Davis for staying in there, and on winning his next two matches over two great players Jeremy Jones and Johnny Archer.

Also, congratulations to Shawn Putnam for winning the Pittsburgh UPA Tour stop! It is Shawn's well-deserved first major win and puts him at number one on tour for the new calendar year 2005 (Shawn went on to win the next tour stop at Valley Forge, making him a rare pro player to win back-to-back tour stops)!

Remember, it's not over till the last ball drops! Stay focused on playing good pool until the end.

SYNCHRONIZED CUE DANCING

Playing pool is like dancing; not only your shooting form, but also your movements in between shots. The way you walk, carry your cue, chalk up, look at the table, line up, and eventually stroke the cue all give clues to how well you play, as well as affect your results on the table.

I think it serves the pool player well to be fluid in action and have rhythm. This could entail graceful, powerful and controlled motions while at the table. You have a unique was of moving your body around the table and stroking your cue. Be like a child. Dance around uninhibited and filled with joy. Be like a ballet dancer. Find freedom and expression in your range of movements. Be like a hunter, focused and stealthy in your approach.

Your positive body language alone will counteract the disabling effects of fear if you have any. Acting indecisively can plant the seed of doubt in your mind, thus causing you to flub a shot. Would you not rather ROCK the shot, ROCK the run out, and ROCK this game?!

Your mind is one with the creator's. Trust yourself and play your game of pool. Act confidently and you will be confident. Act smoothly and you will be smooth. Act unflappably and you will be unflappable.

Stay down and keep your eye on the ball and you will run out. Dance around the table and you will dance the balls into the pockets!

TAKING INVENTORY

In many past articles, I've focused on the fundamental mechanics of playing solid pool. Much of the information I have given has been in the shape of principles as they relate to alignment, aiming, stroke, and mental effectiveness.

Hopefully, some of the ideas, tips, and "secrets" I have given you have provided benefit to your game.

The fact that we are all a little different in form and ability, and the fact that there are players who have success with many different styles proves that there is no ONE way of playing pool right. However, tried and true fundamentals hold up over time and under pressure, and one can often find benefit in working to make his own technique simpler, more effective, and to the point.

Usually, the proof is in the pudding. The litmus test of your game is in your results; the ability that you can consistently display and in the high points you can reach. Your low points or slumps are useful in showing you what could use improvement in your game.

So in this article, I will not teach you a new tip or secret; rather I will give you a list of questions for you to ask yourself that could help you assess the current state of your game, and help push you in the right direction to make intelligent improvements.

I'm sure you have heard that it can often be the questions we ask ourselves that help take us to the next level in anything we do. So I've created a list of questions for you that relate to different aspects of your pool game. If you cannot answer these questions off the top of your mind, just go to the table and find out the answers.

Maybe you will find that you are a pool virtuoso, or what you might need to improve on your path to becoming one. Challenge one of your pool room friends with these questions if you want. You can also add to this list of questions to further increase your awareness of yourself, and your relation to the many aspects of this game we call pool.

AIM

1. Can you find the contact point?
2. Can you find the aiming (stroking) line?
3. Can you set up your stance and stroke on the aiming line?
4. Can you adjust you aim accurately for throw and deflection?

ROTATION (Spin)

1. Can you judge the correct amount of spin to get the cue ball going in the direction you want off of object balls, rails, or the flat bed of the table such as a curve shot?
2. Can you deliver the cue tip to the chosen spot on the cue ball?
3. Can you apply the spin effectively with your stroke?

FORCE (Speed)

1. Are you choosing a destination for the cue ball before you set your stance?
2. Can you judge your needed speed?
3. Can you execute the speed you have chosen?
4. Can you adjust to new equipment and changing playing conditions?

STROKE

1. Can you deliver your cue (stroke) on the aiming line?
2. Can you hit the cue ball with no side spin?
3. Do you follow through?
4. Are you smooth?

FUNDAMENTALS

1. Do your mechanics get the job done?
2. Does your body interfere with your stroke on your follow-through?
3. Are you in control of your body, or do you jump up during your stroke?
4. Are your bridges solid?

STRATEGY

1. Do you plan your whole run out in advance?
2. Do you precisely plan your cue ball and object ball paths?
3. Do you always think at least two balls ahead of your current shot?
4. Do you know many different ways to achieve position from a singe shot?

MENTAL GAME

1. Do you have positive self talk?
2. Do you play with confidence?
3. Do you always try 100% no matter what the score is?
4. Do you get down on yourself when you are playing bad, or just keep trying hard until you get your game back?
5. Do you put yourself in tough matches to expand your comfort zone?

Well, I hope you can find some of these questions useful on your path to self improvement in your pool game and also in life. Stay focused, enjoy the game, and keep making the next ball and playing position!

Max Eberle

Here is a Max Eberle original painting, acrylic on canvas, about five feet tall, and glows in the black light. The subject matter is Michael Jordan, who has inspired athletes in all sports, and whose name has become synonymous with greatness. One great thing about him is that he was known for playing hard even in practice. Practicing with passion in pool will do wonders for your own game.

RECOMMENDED WEBSITES

www.maxeberle.com

Pool Related:

www.insidepoolmag.com
www.azbilliards.com
www.aaabilliards.com
www.hollywoodbilliards.com
www.propoolvideo.com
www.onthewirebilliards.com
www.cuetable.com
www.billiardaimtrainer.com
www.accueshot.com

Personal Interest:

www.golddealer.com
www.organicconsumers.org
www.skinnybitch.net
www.themeatrix.com
www.peta.com
www.happycow.net
www.dragonherbs.com

"Nothing will benefit health or increase chances of survival of life on Earth as the evolution to a vegetarian diet."
Albert Einstein

"Nonviolence is the greatest force at the disposal of mankind. It is mightier than the mightiest weapon of destruction devised by the ingenuity of mankind."
Mahatma Gandhi

ABOUT THE AUTHOR

Max Eberle was born in Dover, Ohio on November 27th, 1972, and taught to play pool by his legendary pool-playing grandfather, Charles Eberle. With the encouragement of his rather, Robert, at twelve years of age, Max decided he would "Go Pro" one day. Max went on to win the National Junior Championships, back-to-back National Collegiate Championships, the 2005 West Coast 9-Ball Championship, and recently was a semi-finalist at the 2006 WPA World Straight Pool Championship, with high runs of 114 and 127-and-out in the quarter finals.

Ranked in the top 5 on the US Pro Circuit in 2003 and 2004, Max has won numerous regional Pro events and has so far won matches against most of the top players and World Champions of today. Voted the 2003 Pro Tour Sportsman of the Year, he has played in events extensively throughout the US, Europe, and Asia. He has given entertaining and educational exhibitions to diverse audiences, and has given free clinics and cues to the children at the Boys and Girls Club and the Sunrise Retirement Home.

Eberle is on call in Los Angeles where he resides, performing and providing technical assistance with movies and commercials, including a Hanes Commercial starring Michael Jordan. Having taught pool for over fifteen years now, Max gives private lessons to pool enthusiasts and celebrities at their homes, or at Hollywood Billiards where he often plays and practices. He has been an instructional columnist for several publications, most notably *Inside Pool Magazine*. Max's high runs on a 9-foot table are: 10 consecutive break and runs in 9-Ball, 15 balls in One-Pocket, and 196 balls in Straight Pool.

Max Eberle has also been an artist since an early age. With the encouragement of his mother, Estelle, Max started his formal art training at five years of age and has since won several awards and had numerous showings. To learn more about Max's artwork, please visit www.maxeberle.com. Max's artistic interests also include drawing, drafting, graphic design, logo design, architectural design, photography, writing poetry and songs, and creating music. Hidden Histories, sacred geometry, astro-theology, symbolic literacy, quantum-physics, nutrition, Chinese tonic herbs, vegan cuisine, Yoga, sports, traveling, and wilderness adventure are also among Max's interests.

Max Eberle